KINGFISHER CHILDREN'S BOOK OF WORDS

GEORGE BEAL

KINGf**ISHER**

KINGFISHER
Kingfisher Publications Plc
New Penderel House, 283–288 High Holborn
London WC1V 7HZ

This edition published by Kingfisher Publications Plc 1999
First published as *Book of Words* by Kingfisher Publications Plc 1991
10 9 8 7 6 5 4 3 2 1

1TR/0799/EDK/HBM(HBM)/125EDI

Copyright © Kingfisher Publications Plc 1991

All rights reserved. No part of this publication may
be reproduced, stored in a retrieval system or
transmitted by any means, electronic, mechanical,
photocopying or otherwise without the prior
permission of the publisher.

A CIP catalogue record of this book is available
from the British Library.

ISBN 0 7534 0414 1

General Editor: John Grisewood
Edited by Nicola Barber
Illustrated by Peter Stevenson (Jillian Burgess Illustrations)
Designed by Robert Wheeler
Phototypeset by Southern Positives and Negatives
(SPAN), Lingfield, Surrey
Printed in Spain

Contents

INTRODUCTION	8
MODERN QUOTATIONS	9
Alphabetical list of people quoted	39
PROVERBS	41
IDIOMS	73
ROOTS	105
American-British word list	130
ORIGINS	137
ENGLISH USAGE	169

Introduction

Although, strictly speaking, English is a Teutonic language, it is also a language of mixed origins. 'Teutonic' means that it is part of that family of Germanic languages which also include German itself, Dutch, Flemish, Frisian, Afrikaans, Swedish, Danish, Norwegian and Icelandic. But English has greatly changed since it was transformed from Anglo-Saxon, or Old English. It has taken words from Latin, French, Greek and many other tongues, which makes it unique among the languages of the world.

As its title suggests, this is a book about words. It tells about the English language, and how many of our words came into that language. *Atlas*, for instance, comes to us from the Greek, and was originally the name of the Titan who held up the sky. *Confetti* comes from Italian, and meant not small pieces of paper, but little sweets.

The book explains how the language is used, and gives help in writing sentences and speaking the language. There is also a part which shows the difference in meaning between the two main varieties of English, American and British, as well as defining those words which are used only in American English or British English.

There are sections listing idioms and proverbs, explaining what they mean. There is a whole section on modern quotations, and who said them. There is help in deciding how words are spelled and there are many examples of how words have changed in meaning. *Paradise*, for instance, once meant 'a royal park', and *silly* meant 'blessed'.

Do you know what an *eponym* is? Or a *homonym*? There are examples of both in the book, as well as anagrams, synonyms, antonyms, acronyms and many others.

GEORGE BEAL

MODERN QUOTATIONS

MODERN QUOTATIONS

Everyone uses quotations in their everyday speech, sometimes without realizing that they are, in fact, quoting the words of someone else. Probably the most-quoted of all people is William Shakespeare. There exist several large volumes which are entirely devoted to quotations from his works. This chapter concentrates on modern quotations, mostly first used in the present century. A key-word system is used to find a particular quotation – for example, if you want to look up who wrote 'O to be in England, now that April's there', you look up **England** and find that the quotation was originated by Robert Browning. If you want to know more about the person quoted you can turn to the alphabetical list at the end of the chapter. The quotations in boxes are, in fact, misquotations.

abnormal
If it weren't for the fact that all of us are slightly abnormal, there wouldn't be any point in giving each person a separate name.
UGO BETTI.

abstract
Abstract art? A product of the untalented, sold by the unprincipled to the utterly bewildered.
AL CAPP.

acting
Acting is not a profession for adults.
LAURENCE OLIVIER.

The general consensus seems to be that I don't act at all.
GARY COOPER.

The hardest kind of acting works only if you look as if you are not acting at all.
HENRY FONDA.

actors
Seventy-five per cent of being successful as an actor is pure luck. The rest is just endurance.
GENE HACKMAN.

Actors and burglars work better at night.
SIR CEDRIC HARDWICKE.

adapting
Human creatures have a marvellous power of adapting themselves to necessity.
GEORGE GISSING.

adults
Adults are obsolete children.
DR SEUSS.

adventure
Adventure is the result of poor planning.
COL. BLASHFORD-SNELL.

advice
No-one wants advice – only corroboration.
JOHN STEINBECK.

alive
It's a funny old world; a man's lucky if he gets out alive.
W.C. FIELDS.

> **alone** I want to be alone. GRETA GARBO. Her true words were: "I like to be alone.".

11

MODERN QUOTATIONS

America
America is God's Crucible, the Great Melting-Pot.
                ISRAEL ZANGWILL.

amused
We are not amused.
                QUEEN VICTORIA.

angels
Angels can fly because they take themselves lightly.
                G.K. CHESTERTON.

antique
An antique is something that's been useless so long it's still in good condition.
                FRANKLIN P. JONES.

applaud
If they liked you, they didn't applaud – they just let you live.
                BOB HOPE.

archaeologist
An archaeologist is the best husband a woman can have; the older she gets the more interested he is in her.
                AGATHA CHRISTIE.

arguing
I am not arguing with you – I am telling you.
                JAMES MCNEILL WHISTLER.

argument
The best way I know to win an argument is to start by being in the right.
                LORD HAILSHAM.
The only way to get the best of an argument is to avoid it.
                DALE CARNEGIE.

armour
Armour is the kind of clothing worn by a man whose tailor was a blacksmith.
                AMBROSE BIERCE.

assassination
Assassination is the extreme form of censorship.
                GEORGE BERNARD SHAW.

atheist
I am an atheist still, thank God.
                LUIS BUÑUEL.
The worst moment for an atheist is when he feels grateful and doesn't know who to thank.
                WENDY WARD.

audience
If all the world's a stage, and all the men and women merely players, where do all the audiences come from?
                DENIS NORDEN.
A work of art does not exist without its audience.
                RICHARD HAMILTON.
The only real teacher of acting is the audience.
                GEORGE C. SCOTT.

average
Most people are such fools that it really is no compliment to say that a man is above average.
                W. SOMERSET MAUGHAM.

MODERN QUOTATIONS

badly
If a thing is worth doing it is worth doing badly.
G.K. CHESTERTON.

ball
The ball is man's most disastrous invention, not excluding the wheel.
ROBERT MORLEY.

bank
Banks lend you money as people lend you an umbrella when the sun is shining and want it back when it starts to rain.
SIR EDWARD BEDDINGTON-BEHRENS.
A bank is a place that will lend you money if you can prove that you don't need it.
BOB HOPE.

bat
Twinkle, twinkle little bat!
How I wonder what you're at!
LEWIS CARROLL.

beard
An irregular greying beard was a decoration to a face which badly needed assistance.
EDGAR WALLACE.
I grew a beard for Nero, in *Quo Vadis*, but Metro-Goldwyn-Mayer thought it didn't look real, so I had to wear a false one.
PETER USTINOV.

beautiful
Remember that the most beautiful things in the world are the most useless; peacocks and lilies for instance.
JOHN RUSKIN.

Bible
The number one book of the ages was written by a committee, and it was called the Bible.
LOUIS B. MAYER.

bigger
The bigger they come, the harder they fall.
ROBERT FITZSIMMONS.

billiards
Proficiency at billiards is proof of a misspent youth.
HERBERT SPENCER.

blind
In the country of the blind the one-eyed man is king.
H.G. WELLS.

MODERN QUOTATIONS

blushing
Man is the only animal that blushes – or needs to.
      MARK TWAIN.

boaster
A boaster is not always a liar.
      ERIC PARTRIDGE.

books
The only books I have in my library are books that other people have lent me.
      ANATOLE FRANCE.

When I am dead, I hope it may be said: "His sins were scarlet, but his books were read."
      HILAIRE BELLOC.

bore
A fellow who talks when you wish him to listen.
      AMBROSE BIERCE.

box
We give people a box in the suburbs. It's called a house, and every night they sit in it staring at another box, in the morning they run off to another box called an office, and at the weekends they get into another box, on wheels this time, and grope their way through endless traffic jams.
      CAROLINE KELLY.

boxing
Boxing is glamorized violence.
      LORD TAYLOR OF GRYFE.

bravery
There is no such thing as bravery; only degrees of fear.
      JOHN WAINWRIGHT.

breakfast
If you want to eat well in England, eat three breakfasts.
      W. SOMERSET MAUGHAM.

brother
I want to be the white man's brother, not his brother-in-law.
      MARTIN LUTHER KING.

buck
The buck stops here.
      HARRY S. TRUMAN (*Sign on President Truman's desk*)

cards
When a man tells me he's going to put all his cards on the table, I always look up his sleeve.
      LORD HORE-BELISHA.

care
If I'd known how old I was going to be I'd have taken better care of myself.
      ADOLPH ZUKOR.

celebrity
A celebrity is a person who works hard all his life to become known, then wears dark glasses to avoid being recognized.
      FRED ALLEN.

cheese
How can you govern a country which produces 246 different kinds of cheese?
CHARLES DE GAULLE.

child
When a child is grown up, it's time the parents learned to stand on their own feet.
FRANCIS HOPE.

cinema
The cinema is not a slice of life. It's a piece of cake.
ALFRED HITCHCOCK.
Cinema is the most beautiful fraud in the world.
JEAN-LUC GODARD.

city
The city is not a concrete jungle, it is a human zoo.
DESMOND MORRIS.

civil servants
Some civil servants are neither servants nor civil.
WINSTON CHURCHILL.

clever
I know I'm not clever, but I'm always right.
J.M. BARRIE.

club
I don't want to belong to any club that will accept me as a member.
GROUCHO MARX.

comeback
I'm always making a comeback, but nobody ever tells me where I've been.
BILLIE HOLLIDAY.

comedian
A comedian does funny things; a good comedian does things funny.
BUSTER KEATON.

comedy
Comedy is simply a funny way of being serious.
PETER USTINOV.
All I need to make a comedy is a park, a policeman and a pretty girl.
CHARLIE CHAPLIN.

comment
Comment is free, but facts are sacred.
C.P. SCOTT.

common man
The century on which we are entering – the century which will come out of this war – can be and must be the century of the common man.
HENRY WALLACE.

composers
Composers should write tunes that chauffeurs and errand boys can whistle.
SIR THOMAS BEECHAM.

MODERN QUOTATIONS

computer
To err is human, but to really foul things up requires a computer.
                              PAUL EHRLICH.

conscience
I cannot and I will not cut my conscience to fit this year's fashions.
                              LILLIAN HELLMAN.

consequences
You can do anything in this world if you are prepared to take the consequences.
                              W. SOMERSET MAUGHAM.

contract
A verbal contract isn't worth the paper it's written on.
                              SAM GOLDWYN.

cook
The cook was a good cook, as cooks go; and as cooks go, she went.
                              'SAKI' (H.H. MUNRO).

courtesy
Courtesy is not dead. It has merely taken refuge in Great Britain.
                              GEORGES DUHAMEL.

cricket
There is one great similarity between music and cricket. There are slow movements in both.
                              NEVILLE CARDUS.

customer
The customer is always right.
                              H. GORDON SELFRIDGE.

cynic
A cynic is a man who knows the price of everything and the value of nothing.
                              OSCAR WILDE.

day
It was such a lovely day I thought it was a pity to get up.
                              W. SOMERSET MAUGHAM.

MODERN QUOTATIONS

dead
What I like about Clive
Is that he is no longer alive.
There is a great deal to be said
For being dead.
> E.C. BENTLEY.

death
I'm not afraid to die; I just don't want to be there when it happens.
> WOODY ALLEN.

After the first death, there is no other.
> DYLAN THOMAS.

I have lost friends, some by death, others through sheer inability to cross the street.
> VIRGINIA WOOLF.

devil
It is stupid of modern civilization to have given up believing in the devil when he is the only explanation of it.
> RONALD KNOX.

diary
Keep a diary and one day it will keep you.
> MAE WEST.

die
To die will be an awfully big adventure.
> J.M. BARRIE.

Die, my dear doctor? That's the last thing I shall do.
> LORD PALMERSTON.

directions
Lord Ronald ... flung himself upon his horse and rode madly off in all directions.
> STEPHEN LEACOCK.

> **discretion** Discretion is the better part of valour. WILLIAM SHAKESPEARE. The correct quotation is: 'The better part of valour is discretion.'.

disgruntled
I could see that, if not actually disgruntled, he was far from being gruntled.
> P.G. WODEHOUSE.

dog
A dog is the only thing on earth that loves you more than you love yourself.
> JOSH BILLINGS.

Any man who hates dogs and babies can't be all bad.
> LEO C. ROSTEN.

The noblest of all dogs is the hot dog; it feeds the hand that bites it.
> LAURENCE J. PETER.

dontopedalogy
Dontopedalogy is the science of opening your mouth and putting your foot in it.
> PRINCE PHILIP (DUKE OF EDINBURGH.)

down and out
When you are down and out something always turns up – and it is usually the noses of your friends.
> ORSON WELLES.

MODERN QUOTATIONS

dreams
But I, being poor, have only my dreams;
I have spread my dreams under your feet;
Tread softly because you tread on my dreams.
W.B. YEATS.

drowning
I was much too far out all my life,
And not waving but drowning.
STEVIE SMITH.

dull
There are no dull subjects. There are only dull writers.
H.L. MENCKEN.

dying
Dying is a very dull, dreary affair. My advice to you is to have nothing whatever to do with it.
W. SOMERSET MAUGHAM.

Dying
Is an art, like everything else.
I do it exceptionally well.
SYLVIA PLATH.

"ALL ANIMALS ARE EQUAL. BUT SOME ANIMALS ARE MORE EQUAL THAN OTHERS."

E

ears
His ears make him look like a taxi with both doors open.
HOWARD HUGHES (referring to Clark Gable).

It's all very well to be able to write books, but can you waggle your ears?
J.M. BARRIE.

earth
The meek shall inherit the earth, but not its mineral rights.
J. PAUL GETTY.

earthquake
What we want is a story that starts with an earthquake and works its way up to a climax.
SAM GOLDWYN.

east
Oh, East is East, and West is West, and never the twain shall meet.
RUDYARD KIPLING.

education
Education has for its object the formation of character.
HERBERT SPENCER.

Education is what survives when what has been learned has been forgotten.
B.F. SKINNER.

MODERN QUOTATIONS

elephant
I have a memory like an elephant. In fact, elephants often consult me.
NOËL COWARD.

enemies
Do not fear when your enemies criticize you. Beware when they applaud.
VO DONG GIANG.

England
That there's some corner of a foreign field
That is for ever England.
RUPERT BROOKE.

Oh, to be in England
Now that April's there.
ROBERT BROWNING.

English
This is the sort of English up with which I will not put.
WINSTON CHURCHILL.

An Englishman, even if he is alone, forms an orderly queue of one.
GEORGE MIKES.

An Englishman thinks he is moral only when he is uncomfortable.
GEORGE BERNARD SHAW.

enjoy
The only way to enjoy anything in this life is to earn it first.
GINGER ROGERS.

equal
All animals are equal, but some animals are more equal than others.
GEORGE ORWELL.

All men are born equal, but quite a few eventually get over it.
LORD MANCROFT.

evolution
Evolution is far more important than living.
ERNST JUNGER.

excuses
Several excuses are always less convincing than one.
ALDOUS HUXLEY.

facts
The trouble with facts is that there are so many of them.
SAMUEL MCCHORD CROTHERS.

Generally, the theories we believe we call facts and the facts we disbelieve we call theories.
FELIX COHEN.

failure
There is much to be said for failure. It is more interesting than success.
MAX BEERBOHM.

There is no formula for success. But there is a formula for failure, and that is trying to please everybody.
NICHOLAS RAY.

fairies
There are fairies at the bottom of our garden!
ROSE FYLEMAN.

famous
It took me fifteen years to discover I had no talent for writing, but I couldn't give it up, because by that time I was too famous.
ROBERT BENCHLEY.

The tragedy of being famous is that you have to devote so much time to being famous.
PABLO PICASSO.

fancy
A little of what you fancy does you good.
MARIE LLOYD.

MODERN QUOTATIONS

fat
Imprisoned in every fat man a thin one is wildly signalling to be let out.
                    CYRIL CONNOLLY.

fate
I am the master of my fate;
I am the captain of my soul.
                    W.E. HENLEY.

Fate keeps on happening.
                    ANITA LOOS.

father
And when did you last see your father?
                    W.F. YEAMES.

fear
The only thing we have to fear is fear itself.
                    FRANKLIN D. ROOSEVELT.

We fear something before we hate it. A child who fears noises becomes a man who hates noises.
                    CYRIL CONNOLLY.

Fear is essential. It is like a drug.
                    LUIS MIGUEL DOMINGUIN.

female
For the female of the species is more deadly than the male.
                    RUDYARD KIPLING.

fence
If the fence is strong enough I'll sit on it.
                    CYRIL SMITH.

few
Never in the field of human conflict was so much owed by so many to so few.
                    WINSTON CHURCHILL (*1940*).

fight
We shall fight on the beaches, we shall fight on the landing grounds, we shall fight in the fields and in the streets, we shall fight in the hills; we shall never surrender.
                    WINSTON CHURCHILL (*1940*).

film
Every film should have a beginning, a middle and an end – but not necessarily in that order.
                    JEAN-LUC GODARD.

A film is never really good unless the camera is an eye in the head of a poet.
                    ORSON WELLES.

firm
I am firm. You are obstinate. He is a pig-headed fool.
                    KATHARINE WHITEHORN.

fisherman
All you need to be a fisherman is patience and a worm.
                    HERB SHRINER.

flowers
Where have all the flowers gone?
The young girls picked them every one.
                    PETE SEEGER.

folk-singer
A folk-singer is someone who sings through his nose by ear.
                                ANON.

food
On the Continent, people have good food; in England people have good table manners.
                        GEORGE MIKES.

football
Some people think football is a matter of life and death. . . . I can assure you it is much more serious than that.
                        BILL SHANKLY.

friend
A friend in need is a friend to be avoided.
                        LORD SAMUEL.

I do not believe that friends are necessarily the people you like best, they are merely the people who got there first.
                        PETER USTINOV.

funny
What do you mean, funny? Funny peculiar or funny ha-ha?
                                IAN HAY.

MODERN QUOTATIONS

future
I have seen the future, and it works.
                        LINCOLN STEFFENS.
I never think of the future. It comes soon enough.
                        ALBERT EINSTEIN.
The best thing about the future is that it only comes one day at a time.
                        DEAN ACHESON.

gamesmanship
Or the Art of Winning Games without Actually Cheating.
                        STEPHEN POTTER.

genius
The genius of Einstein leads to Hiroshima.
                        PABLO PICASSO.
Genius is one per cent inspiration and ninety-nine per cent perspiration.
                        THOMAS A. EDISON.

MODERN QUOTATIONS

gentleman
The English country gentleman galloping after a fox – the unspeakable in full pursuit of the uneatable.
OSCAR WILDE.

gluttony
"What I like about gluttony," a bishop I once knew used to say, "is that it doesn't hurt anyone else."
MONICA FURLONG.

goal
You've got a goal. I've got a goal. Now all we need is a football team.
GROUCHO MARX.

golf
Golf is a game whose aim is to hit a very small ball into an even smaller hole, with weapons singularly ill-designed for the purpose.
WINSTON CHURCHILL.

good
On the whole human beings want to be good, but not too good, and not quite all the time.
GEORGE ORWELL.

goodness
Goodness is easier to recognize than to define.
W.H. AUDEN.

gourmet
A gourmet is just a glutton with brains.
PHILIP W. HABERMAN JR.

greatest
I am the greatest.
MUHAMMAD ALI.

grown-ups
One of the most obvious facts about grown-ups to a child is that they have forgotten what it is like to be a child.
RANDALL JARRELL.

guest
The art of being a good guest is to know when to leave.
PRINCE PHILIP (DUKE OF EDINBURGH).

guilty
It is better that ten guilty persons escape than one innocent suffer.
SIR WILLIAM BLACKSTONE.

H

haircut
Don't ask the barber whether you need a haircut.
                    DANIEL S. GREENBERG.

happiness
One should never let one's happiness depend on other people.
                    H. GRANVILLE BARKER.
Only in romantic novels are the beautiful guaranteed happiness.
                    LADY CYNTHIA ASQUITH.
There is no such thing as the pursuit of happiness, but there is the discovery of joy.
                    JOYCE GRENFELL.

happy
Even if we can't be happy, we must always be cheerful.
                    IRVING KRISTOL.

hatchet
No one ever forgets where he buried the hatchet.
                    KIM HUBBARD.

health
Too much health is unhealthy.
                    LEO C. ROSTEN.

healthy
Early to rise and early to bed
Makes a male healthy, wealthy and dead.
                    JAMES THURBER.

heaven
If you go to Heaven without being naturally qualified for it, you will not enjoy yourself there.
                    GEORGE BERNARD SHAW.

hell
In hell there is no other punishment than to begin over and over again the tasks left unfinished in your lifetime.
                    ANDRÉ GIDE.

heroes
People are only heroes when they cannot do anything else.
                    PAUL CLAUDEL.

hesitates
He who hesitates is sometimes saved.
                    JAMES THURBER.

historian
The novelist is the historian of the present. The historian is the novelist of the past.
                    GEORGES DUHAMEL.

history
History, Stephen said, is a nightmare from which I am trying to awake.
                    JAMES JOYCE.
History is an endless repetition of the wrong way of living.
                    LAWRENCE DURRELL.
History teaches us that men and nations behave wisely once they have exhausted all other alternatives.
                    ABBA EBAN.
The history of the world is the record of a man in quest of his daily bread and butter.
                    H.W. VAN LOON.

Hitler
Hitler was a profoundly *uneducated* man of genius; there could be nothing more dangerous ...
                    A.L. ROWSE.

hole
A hole is nothing at all, but you can break your neck on it.
                    AUSTIN O'MALLEY.

holidays
Term, holidays, term, holidays, till we leave school, and then work, work, work till we die.
C.S. LEWIS.

Hollywood
Hollywood – a place where the inmates are in charge of the asylum.
LAURENCE STALLINGS.

home
Too many young people are beginning to regard home as a filling station by day and a parking place for the night.
REV. WILLIAM JOYCE.

hope
A poet's hope: to be, like some valley cheese, local, but prized elsewhere.
W.H. AUDEN.

horse
A horse is dangerous at both ends and uncomfortable in the middle.
IAN FLEMING.

host
The happy host makes a sad guest.
HAROLD ACTON.

house
A house is a machine for living in.
LE CORBUSIER.

human
A human being: an ingenious assembly of portable plumbing.
CHRISTOPHER MORLEY.

The human species is, to some extent, the result of mistakes which arrested our development and prevented us from assuming the somewhat unglamorous form of our primitive ancestors.
JONATHAN MILLER.

humour
Humour is practically the only thing about which the English are utterly serious.
MALCOLM MUGGERIDGE.

I have a fine sense of the ridiculous, but no sense of humour.
EDWARD ALBEE.

ill
One of the minor pleasures of life is to be slightly ill.
HAROLD NICOLSON.

influence
How to win friends and influence people.
DALE CARNEGIE.

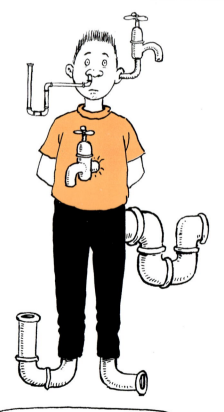

AN INGENIOUS ASSEMBLY OF PORTABLE PLUMBING.

MODERN QUOTATIONS

J

jazz
What they call jazz is just the music of people's emotions.
WILLIE 'THE LION' SMITH.

joke
A joke isn't a joke until someone laughs.
MICHAEL CRAWFORD.

journalists
Journalists say a thing they know isn't true, in the hope that if they keep on saying it long enough it *will* be true.
ARNOLD BENNETT.

justice
Justice should not only be done, but should manifestly and undoubtedly be seen to be done.
LORD HEWART.

K

kids
There are three ways to get something done; do it yourself, hire someone, or forbid your kids to do it.
MONTA CRANE.

killed
Was it you or your brother who was killed in the war?
REV. WILLIAM SPOONER.

kills
Wild animals never kill for sport. Man is the only one to whom the torture and death of his fellow creatures is amusing in itself.
J.A. FROUDE.

kleptomaniac
A kleptomaniac is someone who helps himself because he can't help himself.
ANON.

MODERN QUOTATIONS

lamps
The lamps are going out all over Europe; we shall not see them lit again in our lifetime.
> VISCOUNT GREY OF FALLODON (*1914*).

laugh
Laugh, and the world laughs with you;
Weep, and you weep alone,
For the sad old earth must borrow its mirth,
But has trouble enough of its own.
> ELLA WHEELER WILCOX.

letting go
It's all right letting yourself go, as long as you can get yourself back.
> MICK JAGGER.

liberty
Liberty is the right to tell people what they do not want to hear.
> GEORGE ORWELL.

lie
If one cannot invent a really convincing lie, it is often better to stick to the truth.
> ANGELA THIRKELL.

> **lie** A lie travels round the world while truth is putting on her boots. REV. C.H. SPURGEON. He was misquoted by James Callaghan, who said: "A lie can be halfway round the world before the truth has got its boots on.".

life
Life is a zoo in a jungle.
> PETER DE VRIES.

light
My candle burns at both ends;
It will not last the night;
But, ah, my foes, and oh my friends –
It gives a lovely light.
> EDNA ST VINCENT MILLAY.

literature
Literature is the art of writing something that will be read twice; journalism what will be grasped at once.
> CYRIL CONNOLLY.

love
Love is a many-splendoured thing.
> HAN SUYIN.

MODERN QUOTATIONS

The paths of love are rougher
Than thoroughfares of stones.
                    THOMAS HARDY.

Love conquers all things except poverty and toothache.
                    MAE WEST.

loved
'Tis better to have loved and lost
Than never to have loved at all.
                    ALFRED, LORD TENNYSON.

luck
We must believe in luck. For how else can we explain the success of those we don't like?
                    JEAN COCTEAU.

lunatic
Every reform movement has a lunatic fringe.
                    THEODORE ROOSEVELT.

mad dogs
Mad dogs and Englishmen go out in the midday sun.
                    NOËL COWARD.

man
Man is a clever animal who behaves like an imbecile.
                    ALBERT SCHWEITZER.

mankind
I love mankind; it's people I can't stand.
                    CHARLES M. SCHULZ.

manners
The reason nobody talks in England is because children are taught manners instead of conversation.
                    ROBERT MORLEY.

mathematics
Mathematics ... possesses not only truth, but supreme beauty – a beauty cold and austere, like that of sculpture.
                    BERTRAND RUSSELL.

memory
Memory is more indelible than ink.
                    ANITA LOOS.

men
Men are like wine – some turn to vinegar, but the best improve with age.
                    POPE JOHN XXIII.

Some of my best leading men have been dogs and horses.
                    ELIZABETH TAYLOR.

mind
The human mind is like an umbrella. It functions best when open.
                    WALTER GROPIUS.

27

money
Money isn't everything: usually it isn't even enough.
                          ANON.

I don't care too much for money,
Money can't buy me love.
                JOHN LENNON AND PAUL McCARTNEY.

> **money** Money is the root of all evil. THE BIBLE, *Timothy, 6:10*. actually reads: 'The love of money is the root of all evil.'.

mother
Nobody can misunderstand a boy like his own mother.
                  NORMAN DOUGLAS.

music
All music is singing. The ideal is to make the orchestra play like singers.
                  BRUNO WALTER.

I don't know anything about music. In my line you don't have to.
                  ELVIS PRESLEY.

I hate music, especially when it's played.
                  JIMMY DURANTE.

Popular music is popular because a lot of people like it.
                  IRVING BERLIN.

my way
I did it my way.
                  PAUL ANKA.

needs
One of the weaknesses of our age is our apparent inability to distinguish our needs from our greeds.
                  DON ROBINSON.

nothing
Nothing matters very much and few things matter at all.
                  LORD BALFOUR.

One of the lessons of history is that nothing is often a good thing to do and always a clever thing to say.
                  WILL DURANT.

novel
This is not a novel to be tossed aside lightly. It should be thrown with great force.
                  DOROTHY PARKER.

number
Well, if I called the wrong number, why did you answer the phone?
                  JAMES THURBER.

old
Anyone can get old. All you have to do is live long enough.
                  GROUCHO MARX.

They shall grow not old, as we that are left grow old.
                  LAURENCE BINYON.

Growing old is something you do if you're lucky.
                  GROUCHO MARX.

It's sad to grow old, but nice to ripen.
                  BRIGITTE BARDOT.

No man is ever old enough to know better.
                  HOLBROOK JACKSON.

old age
Old age is always 15 years older than I am.
                  BERNARD BARUCH.

I prefer old age to the alternative.
                  MAURICE CHEVALIER.

MODERN QUOTATIONS

opera
Nobody really sings in an opera. They just make loud noises.
AMELITA GALLI-CURCI.

optimist
The optimist proclaims that we live in the best of all possible worlds; and the pessimist fears this is true.
JAMES BRANCH CABELL.

overtakers
It's the overtakers who keep the undertakers busy.
WILLIAM PITTS.

pains
I can sympathize with people's pains, but not with their pleasures.
ALDOUS HUXLEY.

paradises
The true paradises are the paradises we have lost.
MARCEL PROUST.

parliament
There are three golden rules for Parliamentary speakers: 'Stand up. Speak up. Shut up.'
J.W. LOWTHER.

past
It's a waste of time thinking hard about the past. There's nothing you can do to change it.
ERTÉ (ROMAIN DE TIRTOFF).
The great thing about the past is that it's happened.
FRANK NORMAN.
The past is a foreign country: they do things differently there.
L.P. HARTLEY.

patience
Patience is not only a virtue. It pays.
B.C. FORBES.

patient
I am extraordinarily patient, provided I get my own way in the end.
MARGARET THATCHER.

pauses
The most precious things in speech are the pauses.
RALPH RICHARDSON.

people
People don't change, they only become more so.
JOHN BRIGHT-HOLMES.
The world is divided into people who do things – and people who get the credit.
DWIGHT MORROW.
Believe me, of all the people in the world, those who want the most are those who have the most.
DAVID GRAYSON.

performance
The only thing you owe to the public is a good performance.
HUMPHREY BOGART.

pessimist
A pessimist is a man who looks both ways when he's crossing a one-way street.
LAURENCE J. PETER.

Philadelphia On the whole, I'd rather be in Philadelphia. W.C. FIELDS. His actual words were "Here lies W.C. Fields. I would rather be living in Philadelphia.". He suggested that this should be engraved on his gravestone but this was not done.

MODERN QUOTATIONS

play
Play it, Sam.
　　　　HUMPHREY BOGART (*in the film* Casablanca).

> **play** "Play it again, Sam." HUMPHREY BOGART, in the film *Casablanca*. In fact, there are two quotations, neither as printed above. The first line was spoken by Ingrid Bergman, who said: "Play it, Sam. Play *As Time Goes By*.". The second line was spoken by Humphrey Bogart, who said: "If she can stand it, I can. Play it.".

poet
A poet is, before anything else, a person who is passionately in love with language.
　　　　W.H. AUDEN.

poetry
There's no money in poetry; but then there's no poetry in money either.
　　　　ROBERT GRAVES.
Poetry is the supreme fiction, madame.
　　　　WALLACE STEVENS.

politician
A politician is an animal that can sit on a fence and keep both ears to the ground.
　　　　H.L. MENCKEN.
The only way a reporter should look at a politician is down.
　　　　FRANK KENT.

politics
Politics is the art of the possible.
　　　　R.A. BUTLER.

pope
Anybody can be Pope; the proof of this is that I have become one.
　　　　POPE JOHN XXIII.

portraits
You don't change the course of history by turning the faces of portraits to the wall.
　　　　JAWAHARLAL NEHRU.

poverty
I worked my way up from nothing to a state of extreme poverty.
　　　　GROUCHO MARX.
Poverty is no disgrace to a man, but it is confoundedly inconvenient.
　　　　SYDNEY SMITH.

MODERN QUOTATIONS

power
Power tends to corrupt, and absolute power corrupts absolutely.
LORD ACTON.

All power is delightful, and absolute power is absolutely delightful.
KENNETH TYNAN.

prayers
Hush! Hush! Whisper who dares!
Christopher Robin is saying his
 prayers.
A.A.MILNE.

president
Anyone who wants to be President should have his head examined.
AVERELL HARRIMAN.

prison
It's not the people in prison who worry me. It's the people who aren't.
EARL OF ARRAN.

prisoner
A prisoner of war is a man who tries to kill you and fails, and then asks you not to kill him.
WINSTON CHURCHILL.

professor
A professor is someone who talks in someone else's sleep.
W.H. AUDEN.

progress
Progress was all right. Only it went on too long.
JAMES THURBER.

qualities
It is not for our faults that we are disliked and even hated, but for our qualities.
BERNARD BERENSON.

quote
I often quote myself. It adds spice to my conversation.
GEORGE BERNARD SHAW.

race
It is not possible to regard our race with anything but alarm. From primeval ooze to the stars, we killed anything that stood in our way, including each other.
GORE VIDAL.

radio
Radio is a creative theatre of the mind.
WOLFMAN JACK SMITH.

rainbow
Somewhere over the rainbow,
Way up high:
There's a land that I heard of
Once in a lullaby.
E.Y. HARBURG.

MODERN QUOTATIONS

rat
The trouble with the rat race is that even if you win, you're still a rat.
    LILY TOMLIN.

reality
Human kind
Cannot bear very much reality.
    T.S. ELIOT.

The dignity of man lies in his ability to face reality in all its meaninglessness.
    MARTIN ESSLIN.

religion
There is only one religion, though there are a hundred versions of it.
    GEORGE BERNARD SHAW.

remember
Those who cannot remember the past are condemned to repeat it.
    GEORGE SANTAYANA.

rich
I have been poor and I have been rich. Rich is better.
    SOPHIE TUCKER.

right
Doing what's right isn't the problem. It's knowing what's right.
    LYNDON B. JOHNSON.

room
All I want is a room somewhere,
Far away from the cold night air.
    ALAN JAY LERNER.

rumours
I hate to spread rumours; but what else can one do with them?
    AMANDA LEAR.

scenery
The scenery was beautiful, but the actors got in front of it.
    ALEXANDER WOOLLCOTT.

school
No one who had any sense ever liked school.
    LORD BOOTHBY.

Shakespeare
I know not, sir, whether Bacon wrote the words of Shakespeare, but if he did not, it seems to me he missed the opportunity of his life.
    J.M. BARRIE.

ship
All I ask is a tall ship and a star to steer her by.
    JOHN MASEFIELD.

show business
There's no business like show business.
    IRVING BERLIN.

MODERN QUOTATIONS

Shredded Wheat
He dreamed he was eating Shredded Wheat and woke up to find the mattress half gone.
FRED ALLEN.

sick
A youth with his first cigar makes himself sick; a youth with his first girl makes other people sick.
MARY WILSON LITTLE.

sitting
Are you sitting comfortably? Then I'll begin.
JULIA LANG.

sixty-four
Will you still need me, will you still feed me,
When I'm sixty-four?
JOHN LENNON AND PAUL McCARTNEY.

small
Small is beautiful.
E.F. SCHUMACHER.

snore
Laugh and the world laughs with you; snore and you sleep alone.
ANTHONY BURGESS.

space
Space isn't remote at all. It's only an hour's drive away if your car could go straight upwards.
SIR FRED HOYLE.

speech
It usually takes me more than three weeks to prepare a good impromptu speech.
MARK TWAIN.

sponge
If I believed in reincarnation, I'd come back as a sponge.
WOODY ALLEN.

stare
What is this life, if full of care,
We have no time to stand and stare?
W.H. DAVIES.

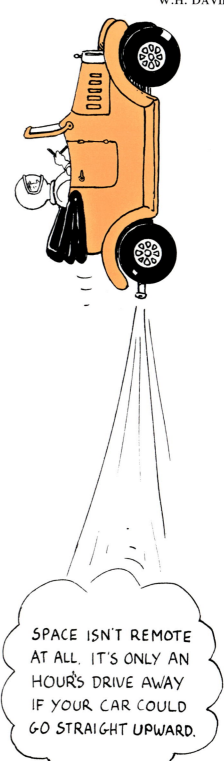

SPACE ISN'T REMOTE AT ALL. IT'S ONLY AN HOUR'S DRIVE AWAY IF YOUR CAR COULD GO STRAIGHT UPWARD.

MODERN QUOTATIONS

stars
Two men look out through the same bars:
One sees the mud, and one the stars.
                FREDERICK LANGBRIDGE.

statesman
A statesman is a politician who's been dead for ten or fifteen years.
                HARRY S. TRUMAN.
When you're abroad, you're a statesman; when you're at home, you're just a politician.
                HAROLD MACMILLAN.

step
That's one small step for a man, one giant leap for mankind.
NEIL A. ARMSTRONG (*The first Moon landing, 1969*).

story-teller
A good story-teller is a person who has a good memory and hopes the others haven't.
                IRWIN S. COBB.

striving
Year by year we are becoming better equipped to accomplish the things we are striving for. But what are we actually striving for?
                BERTRAND DE JOUVENAL.

stupidity
Stupidity is mainly just a lack of capacity to take things in.
                CLIVE JAMES.

style
Style is knowing who you are, what you want to say, and not giving a damn.
                GORE VIDAL.

succeed
It is not enough to succeed. Others must fail.
                GORE VIDAL.

success
The common idea that success spoils people by making them vain, egotistic and self-complacent is erroneous – on the contrary it makes them, for the most part, humble, tolerant and kind. Failure makes people bitter and cruel.
                W. SOMERSET MAUGHAM.
The toughest thing about success is that you've got to keep on being a success.
                IRVING BERLIN.

survival
Survival of the fittest.
                HERBERT SPENCER.

tact
Tact consists in knowing how to go too far.
                JEAN COCTEAU.

MODERN QUOTATIONS

talent
Talent is the least important thing a performer needs, but humility is the one thing he must have.
>CLARK GABLE.

taxidermist
A tall, drooping man, looking as if he had been stuffed in a hurry by an incompetent taxidermist.
>P.G. WODEHOUSE.

tears
I have nothing to offer but blood, toil, tears and sweat.
>WINSTON CHURCHILL (*1940*).

television
Television is an invention that permits you to be entertained in your own living-room by people you wouldn't have in your home.
>DAVID FROST.

Television is for appearing on, not looking at.
>NOËL COWARD.

TV is an evil medium. It should never have been invented, but since we have to live with it, let us try to do something about it.
>RICHARD BURTON.

Why should people pay good money to go out and see bad films when they can stay at home and see bad television for nothing?
>SAM GOLDWYN.

temptation
I can resist everything except temptation.
>OSCAR WILDE.

The last temptation is the greatest treason:
To do the right deed for the wrong reason.
>T.S. ELIOT.

things
It was great fun,
But it was just one of those things.
>COLE PORTER.

time
Time goes, you say? Ah no!
Alas, Time stays, *we* go.
>AUSTIN DOBSON.

Time present and time past
Are both perhaps present in time future
And time future contained in time past.
>T.S. ELIOT.

Modern man thinks he loves something – time – when he does not do things quickly. Yet he does not know what to do with the time he gains – except kill it.
>ERICH FROMM.

So little time, so little to do.
>OSCAR LEVANT.

MODERN QUOTATIONS

tongue
Fighting is essentially a masculine idea; a woman's weapon is her tongue.
HERMIONE GINGOLD.

tools
Give us the tools and we'll finish the job.
WINSTON CHURCHILL.

toothpaste
Once the toothpaste is out of the tube, it's hard to get it back in.
H.R. HALDEMAN.

tragedy
It is the tragedy of the world that no-one knows what he doesn't know; and the less a man knows, the more sure he is that he knows everything.
JOYCE CARY.

train
The only way of catching a train I ever discovered is to miss the train before.
G.K. CHESTERTON.

tree
I think that I shall never see
A poem lovely as a tree.
JOYCE KILMER.

troubles
Pack up your troubles in your old kit-bag.
GEORGE ASAF.

truth
In seeking truth you have to get both sides of a story.
WALTER CRONKITE.
It has always been desirable to tell the truth, but seldom, if ever, necessary.
A.J. BALFOUR.
The first casualty when war comes is truth.
HIRAM JOHNSON.
The truth is rarely pure, and never simple.
OSCAR WILDE.

Truth is a rare and precious commodity.
We must be sparing in its use.
C.P. SCOTT.
Truth may be stranger than fiction, but fiction is truer.
FREDERIC RAPHAEL.

uncertainty
A little uncertainty is good for everyone.
HENRY KISSINGER.

unhappiness
Unhappiness is defined as the difference between our talents and our expectations.
EDWARD DE BONO.

unhappy
All happy families resemble one another, but each unhappy family is unhappy in its own way.
LEO TOLSTOY.

value
What you really value is what you miss, not what you have.
JORGE LUIS BORGES.

Venice
Venice is like eating an entire box of chocolate liqueurs at one go.
TRUMAN CAPOTE.

violence
Violence is the repartee of the illiterate.
ALAN BRIEN.

MODERN QUOTATIONS

walks
I like long walks, especially when they are taken by people who annoy me.
                FRED ALLEN.

waltzing
And he sang as he sat and waited for his billy-boil,
'You'll come a-waltzing, Matilda, with me.'
                A.B. PATERSON.

wanting
As soon as you stop wanting something, you get it.
                ANDY WARHOL.

war
It is better to win the peace and to lose the war.
                BOB MARLEY.

In war, you don't have to be nice, you only have to be right.
                WINSTON CHURCHILL.

Mankind must put an end to war or war will put an end to mankind.
                JOHN F. KENNEDY.

The quickest way of ending a war is to lose it.
                GEORGE ORWELL.

War is fear cloaked in courage.
                GENERAL WILLIAM WESTMORELAND.

water
You can analyse a glass of water and you're left with a lot of chemical components, but nothing you can drink.
                J.B.S. HALDANE.

west
     Go West, young man, Go West!
                J.L.B. SOULE.

whimper
This is the way the world ends
Not with a bang but a whimper.
                T.S. ELIOT.

wind
The wind of change is blowing through the continent.
                HAROLD MACMILLAN.

winter
Now is the winter of our discontent made glorious summer by central heating.
                JACK SHARKEY.

A cold coming we had of it,
Just the worst time of the year
For a journey, and such a long journey:
The ways deep and the weather sharp,
The very dead of winter.
                T.S. ELIOT.

wisdom
Wisdom is knowing when you can't be wise.
                PAUL ENGLE.

women
I hate women because they always know where things are.
                JAMES THURBER.

There are no ugly women, only lazy ones.
                HELENA RUBINSTEIN.

Whatever women do they must do twice as well as men to be thought half as good.
                CHARLOTTE WHITTON.

Women are really much nicer than men. No wonder we like them.
                KINGSLEY AMIS.

wood
People love chopping wood. In this activity one immediately sees results.
                ALBERT EINSTEIN.

MODERN QUOTATIONS

woodshed
Something nasty in the woodshed.
STELLA GIBBONS.

work
I never forget that work is a curse – which is why I've never made it a habit.
BLAISE CENDRARS.

Work expands so as to fill the time available for its completion.
C. NORTHCOTE PARKINSON.

workers
The workers have nothing to lose but their chains. They have a world to gain. Workers of the world unite!
KARL MARX.

world
You have to have some order in a disordered world.
FRANK LLOYD WRIGHT.

Wren, Sir Christopher
Sir Christopher Wren
Said 'I am going to dine with some men.
If anyone calls
Say I'm designing St Paul's.'
E.C. BENTLEY.

writer
It is by sitting down to write every morning that one becomes a writer. Those who do not do this remain amateurs.
GERALD BRENAN.

If a writer disbelieves what he is writing, then he can hardly expect his reader to believe it.
JORGE LUIS BORGES.

writers
Writers should be read; but neither seen nor heard.
DAPHNE DU MAURIER.

wrong
Two wrongs don't make a right, but they make a good excuse.
THOMAS SZASZ.

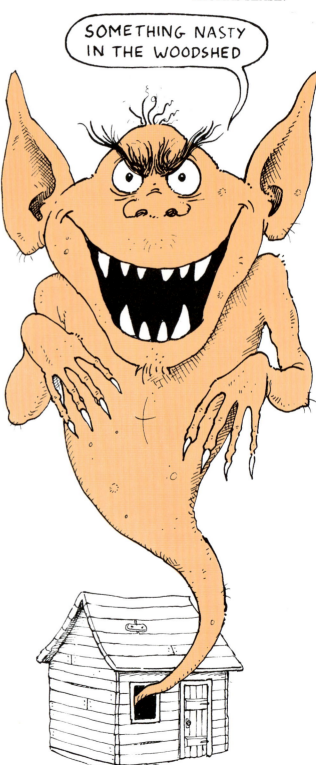

If you want to know who any of the people quoted in this chapter are, you can look them up in the following, alphabetically-arranged list.

Dean Acheson, politician (1893–1971)
Sir Harold Acton, man of letters (1904–)
Lord Acton (Sir J.E.E. Dalberg), historian (1834–1902)
Edward Albee, playwright (1928–)
Fred Allen, comedian (1894–1956)
Woody Allen, actor (1935–)
Muhammad Ali, boxer (1942–)
Kingsley Amis, author (1922–)
Paul Anka, singer (1941–)
Neil A. Armstrong, astronaut (1930–)
Earl of Arran, journalist (1910–1983)
George Asaf, songwriter (1880–1951)
Lady Cynthia Asquith, hostess (1887–1960)
W.H. Auden, poet (1907–1973)
A.J. Balfour, politician (1848–1930)
Brigitte Bardot, film actress (1934–)
J.M. Barrie, playwright (1860–1937)
Bernard Baruch, financier (1870–1965)
Sir Edward Beddington-Behrens, lawyer & statesman (1897–1968)
Sir Thomas Beecham, conductor (1879–1961)
Max Beerbohm, author (1872–1956)
Hilaire Belloc, author (1870–1953)
Robert Benchley, humorist (1889–1945)
Arnold Bennett, author (1867–1931)
E.C. Bentley, writer (1875–1956)
Bernard Berenson, art historian (1865–1959)
Irving Berlin, songwriter (1888–1989)
Ugo Betti, playwright (1892–1953)
Ambrose Bierce, author (1842–1914)
Josh Billings, humorist (1818–1885)
Laurence Binyon, poet (1869–1943)
Sir William Blackstone, lawyer (1723–1780)
Col. Blashford-Snell, soldier (1936–)
Humphrey Bogart, film actor (1899–1957)
Lord Boothby, politician (1900–1986)
Jorge Luis Borges, writer (1899–1986)
Gerald Brenan, writer (1894–1987)
Alan Brien, writer (1925–)
John Bright-Holmes, publisher, (current)
Rupert Brooke, poet (1887–1915)
Robert Browning, poet (1812–1889)
Luis Buñuel, film director (1900–1983)
Anthony Burgess, author (1917–)
Richard Burton, actor (1925–1984)
R.A. Butler, statesman (1902–1982)
James Branch Cabell, novelist (1879–1958)
James Callaghan, statesman (1912–)
Truman Capote, author (1924–1984)
Al Capp, cartoonist (1909–1979)
Neville Cardus, writer (1889–1975)
Dale Carnegie, writer (1888–1955)
Lewis Carroll, writer (1832–1898)
Joyce Cary, British novelist (1888–1957)
Blaise Cendrars, novelist (1887–1961)
Charlie Chaplin, film actor & producer (1889–1977)
G.K. Chesterton, author (1874–1936)
Maurice Chevalier, actor & singer (1888–1972)
Agatha Christie, author (1891–1976)
Winston Churchill, statesman (1874–1965)
Paul Claudel, composer (1868–1955)
Irwin S. Cobb, author (1876–1944)
Jean Cocteau, writer & film director (1889–1963)
Cyril Connolly, writer (1903–1974)
Gary Cooper, film actor (1901–1961)
Noël Coward, actor, composer & director (1898–1973)
Michael Crawford, actor (1942–)
Walter Cronkite, newspaper columnist (1916–)
W.H. Davies, poet (1871–1940)

Edward de Bono, lecturer in medicine (1933–)
Charles de Gaulle, statesman (1890–1970)
Peter de Vries, writer (1910–)
Austin Dobson, poet (1840–1921)
Luis Miguel Dominguin, Spanish bullfighter
Norman Douglas, author (1886–1952)
Georges Duhamel, writer (1884–1966)
Daphne du Maurier, novelist (1907–1989)
Will Durant, historian (1885–1981)
Jimmy Durante, comedian (1893–1980)
Lawrence Durrell, author (1912–1990)
Abba Eban, statesman (1915–)
Thomas A. Edison, inventor (1847–1931)
Paul Ehrlich, scientist (1932–)
Albert Einstein, mathematician (1879–1955)
T.S. Eliot, poet & author (1888–1965)
Paul Engle, poet (1908–)
Erté (Romain de Tirtoff), designer (1892–1990)
Martin Esslin, writer (1918–)
W.C. Fields, actor & comedian (1880–1946)
Robert Fitzsimmons, boxer (1862–1917)
Ian Fleming, novelist (1908–1964)
Henry Fonda, actor (1905–1982)
B.C. Forbes, publisher (1880–1954)
Anatole France, author (1844–1924)
Erich Fromm, psychologist (1900–1980)
David Frost, TV presenter (1939–)
J.A. Froude (1818–1894)
Monica Furlong, novelist (1930–)
Rose Fyleman, writer (1877–1957)
Clark Gable, film actor (1901–1961)
Amelita Galli-Curci, singer (1889–1963)
J. Paul Getty, financier (1892–1976)
Stella Gibbons, novelist (1902–1989)
Andre Gide, writer (1869–1951)
W.S. Gilbert, playwright (1836–1911)
Hermione Gingold, actress (1897–1987)
George Gissing, novelist (1857–1903)
Jean-Luc Godard, film director (1930–)
Sam Goldwyn, film producer (1882–1974)
H. Granville-Barker, actor-manager (1877–1946)
Robert Graves, poet & writer (1895–1986)
David Grayson, journalist & author (1870–1946)
Daniel S. Greenberg, science writer (1931–)
Joyce Grenfell, entertainer (1910–1980)
Viscount Grey of Fallodon, statesman (1884–1916)
Walter Gropius, architect (1883–1969)
Gene Hackman, film actor (1930–)
Lord Hailsham (Quintin Hogg), statesman (1907–)
J.B.S. Haldane, scientist (1892–1964)
H.R. Haldeman, US official (1926–)
Alex Hamilton, journalist (1917–)
Richard Hamilton, artist (1922–)
E.Y. Harburg, lyricist (1896–1981)
Sir Cedric Hardwicke, actor (1893–1964)
Thomas Hardy, novelist (1840–1928)
Averell Harriman, statesman (1891–1986)
L.P. Hartley, novelist (1895–1972)
Ian Hay, novelist (1876–1952)
Lillian Hellman, playwright (1907–1984)
W.E. Henley, poet & playwright (1849–1903)
Lord Hewart, judge (1870–1943)
Alfred Hitchcock, film director (1899–1980)
Billie Holliday, singer (1915–1959)
Bob Hope, comedian (1904–)
Lord Hore-Belisha, statesman (1893–1957)
Sir Fred Hoyle, astronomer (1915–`)
Wilfred Hyde White, actor (1903–)
Aldous Huxley, novelist (1894–1963)

Holbrook Jackson, writer (1874–1978)
Mick Jagger, singer (1943–)
Clive James, TV presenter (1939–)
Randall Jarrell, critic (1914–1965)
Pope John XXIII (1881–1963)
Hiram Johnson, politician (1866–1945)
Lyndon B. Johnson, politician (1908–1973)
James Joyce, novelist (1882–1941)
Ernst Junger, writer (1895–)
Buster Keaton, comedian (1895–1966)
John F. Kennedy, statesman (1917–1963)
Frank Kent, journalist (1907–1978)
Joyce Kilmer, poet (1886–1918)
Martin Luther King, religious leader (1929–1968)
Rudyard Kipling, author (1865–1936)
Henry Kissinger, statesman (1923–)
Ronald Knox, priest & author (1888–1957)
Irving Kristol, academic (1920–)
Julia Lang, actress & broadcaster (1921–)
Frederick Langbridge, priest, poet & playwright (1849–1923)
Stephen Leacock, humorous writer (1869–1944)
Le Corbusier (Charles Edouard Jeanneret), French architect (1881–1965)
John Lennon, singer (1941–1980)
Alan Jay Lerner, playwright (1918–1986)
Oscar Levant, musician (1906–1972)
C.S. Lewis, novelist (1898–1963)
Marie Lloyd, comedienne (1870–1922)
Anita Loos, author (1893–1981)
J.W. Lowther, speaker of the House of Commons (1855–1949)
Paul McCartney, singer & composer (1942–)
Harold Macmillan, statesman (1894–1988)
Lord Mancroft, politician (1914–)
Bob Marley, singer (1945–1981)
Groucho Marx, comedian (1895–1977)
Karl Marx, political theorist (1818–1883)
John Masefield, poet & author (1878–1967)
W. Somerset Maugham, novelist (1874–1965)
Louis B. Mayer, film producer (1885–1957)
H.L. Mencken, journalist & author (1880–1956)
George Mikes, author (1912–)
Edna St Vincent Millay, American poet (1892–1950)
Jonathan Miller, doctor, writer & producer (1936–)
A.A. Milne, author (1882–1956)
Christopher Morley, playwright (1890–1957)
Robert Morley, actor (1908–)
Desmond Morris, author & naturalist (1928–)
Dwight Morrow, lawyer & diplomat (1873–1931)
Malcolm Muggeridge, journalist (1903–1990)
H.H. Munro – see 'Saki'
Jawaharlal Nehru, statesman (1889–1964)
Harold Nicolson, politician (1886–1968)
Denis Norden, writer & broadcaster (1922–)
Frank Norman, author (1930–1980)
Conor Cruise O'Brien, editor (1917–)
Laurence Olivier (Lord Olivier), actor (1907–1989)
Baroness Orczy, novelist (1865–1947)
George Orwell, novelist & essayist (1903–1950)
Lord Palmerston, statesman (1784–1865)
Dorothy Parker, writer (1893–1967)
C. Northcote Parkinson, writer (1909–)
Eric Partridge, lexicographer (1894–1979)
A.B. Paterson, writer (1864–1961)
Prince Philip (Duke of Edinburgh), (1921–)
Pablo Picasso, painter (1881–1973)
Sylvia Plath, poet (1932–1968)
Cole Porter, composer & lyricist (1891–1964)
Stephen Potter, writer (1900–1969)
Elvis Presley, singer (1935–1977)
Marcel Proust, novelist (1871–1922)
Frederic Raphael, novelist (1931–)
Nicholas Ray, film director (1911–)
Ralph Richardson, actor (1902–1983)

Ginger Rogers, film actress (1911–)
Franklin D. Roosevelt, statesman (1882–1945)
Theodore Roosevelt, statesman (1858–1919)
Leo C. Rosten, writer (1908–)
A.L. Rowse, academic (1903–)
Helena Rubinstein, beautician (1872–1965)
John Ruskin, poet & critic (1819–1900)
Bertrand Russell, philosopher (1872–1970)
'Saki' (H.H. Munro), novelist (1870–1916)
Lord Samuel, statesman (1870–1963)
George Santayana, philosopher (1863–1952)
Charles M. Schulz, cartoonist (1922–)
E.F. Schumacher, economist (1911–1977)
Albert Schweitzer, doctor & missionary (1875–1965)
C.P. Scott, journalist (1846–1932)
George C. Scott, film actor (1926–)
Pete Seeger, singer (1919–)
H. Gordon Selfridge, store owner (1864–1947)
Robert Service, poet (1874–1958)
Dr Theodor Seuss, writer (1904–)
Bill Shankly, soccer manager (1918–1981)
George Bernard Shaw, playwright (1856–1950)
B.F. Skinner, American psychiatrist (1904–)
Stevie Smith, poet (1902–1971)
Sydney Smith, clergyman & essayist (1771–1845)
Willie 'The Lion' Smith, jazz musician (1895–1973)
Wolfman Jack Smith, disc jockey
J.L.B. Soule, editor & author (1815–1891)
Herbert Spencer, philosopher (1820–1903)
Laurence Stallings, writer (1894–1968)
Lincoln Steffens, journalist (1866–1936)
John Steinbeck, novelist (1902–1968)
Wallace Stevens, poet (1879–1955)
Han Suyin, novelist (1917–)
Thomas Szasz, psychiatrist (1920–)
Elizabeth Taylor, film actress (1932–)
Lord Taylor of Gryfe, businessman (1912–)
Alfred, Lord Tennyson, poet (1809–1892)
Margaret Thatcher, stateswoman (1925–)
Angela Thirkell, author (1890–1961)
Dylan Thomas, poet (1914–1953)
James Thurber, humorist & cartoonist (1894–1961)
Leo Tolstoy, novelist (1828–1910)
Lily Tomlin, comedienne (1939–)
Harry S. Truman, statesman (1884–1972)
Sophie Tucker, entertainer (1884–1966)
Mark Twain, novelist (1835–1910)
Kenneth Tynan, critic (1927–1980)
Peter Ustinov, actor, author & playwright (1921–)
H.W. Van Loon, author (1882–1944)
Queen Victoria (1819–1901)
Gore Vidal, author (1925–)
Edgar Wallace, novelist (1875–1932)
Henry Wallace, politician (1888–1965)
Bruno Walter, musician (1876–1962)
Andy Warhol, artist & film-maker (1926–1988)
Orson Welles, actor & director (1915–1985)
H.G. Wells, novelist (1886–1946)
Mae West, film actress (1893–1980)
Gen. William Westmoreland, soldier (1914–)
James McNeill Whistler, artist (1834–1903)
Charlotte Whitton, writer (1896–1975)
Ella Wheeler Wilcox, poet (1850–1919)
Oscar Wilde, playwright (1854–1900)
Harry Williams, songwriter (1874–1924)
P.G. Wodehouse, novelist & lyricist (1881–1975)
Tom Wolfe, writer (1931–)
Virginia Woolf, novelist (1882–1941)
Alexander Woollcott, critic (1887–1943)
Frank Lloyd Wright, architect (1869–1959)
W.F. Yeames, painter (1835–1918)
W.B. Yeats, poet (1865–1939)
Israel Zangwill, playwright & novelist (1864–1926)
Adolph Zukor. film producer (1873–1976)

PROVERBS

PROVERBS

Proverbs are short, pithy sayings that contain some wisdom or observation on life and people. Many are familiar, such as *He who hesitates is lost* or *A rolling stone gathers no moss*. Some sound profound, but beware of always believing the wisdom of a proverb. Proverbs are not always right or true! Many proverbs contradict others: *Too many cooks spoil the broth* sounds a sensible statement, and so does *Many hands make light work*, yet they each put forward an opposing idea. So you should always be cautious when using proverbs in speaking or writing.

absence
Absence makes the heart grow fonder. You feel friendlier to your friends when away from them.

accidents
Accidents will happen in the best regulated families. Accidents happen to everyone.

accuse
He who excuses himself accuses himself. Anyone who makes a lot of excuses probably knows that they are in the wrong.

accused
Don't ask for pardon before you're accused. Wait till someone says you're guilty before you make excuses.

accuser
A guilty conscience needs no accuser. If you believe yourself guilty, you have accused yourself.

acorn
Great oaks from little acorns grow. Small or humble origins don't mean that you can't reach the top.
Every oak has been an acorn. Things which start small can become large and important.

adversity
Adversity makes a man wise, not rich. Misfortune may not lead to riches, but it teaches you good lessons.
Prosperity makes friends, adversity tries them. Those who stay friends with you when you're poor are your real friends.
Sweet are the uses of adversity. Misfortune is often a blessing in disguise.

advice
Advice when most needed is least heeded. People who need advice are often the most likely to scorn it.
If you seek advice, ask an old man. Those with experience are likely to have greater wisdom.
Nothing is so freely given as advice. People who do not seek advice themselves, are often the first to offer it.

affairs
There is a tide in the affairs of men. A golden opportunity will probably present itself only once.

affection
Affection blinds reason. Love often leads people to do foolish things.

after
After a storm comes a calm. When things are bad you can nevertheless look forward to better times.
After dinner sit awhile; after supper walk a mile. Rest after a heavy meal, take exercise after a light one.

PROVERBS

age
The golden age was the never present age. People always look to the past for the best times. The present day is never ideal.

agree
Birds in their little nests agree. A happy home is one where there is harmony.

all
All's well that ends well. It's the final outcome that matters, despite what happens on the way.
All good things come to an end. No pleasures go on for ever.
All in the day's work. Good and bad, whatever happens is part of life.
All things are difficult before they're easy. However hard a problem appears to be, perseverance will bring its reward.

alone
He travels fastest who travels alone. An ambitious person is more likely to succeed when unencumbered by others.

angels
Fools rush in where angels fear to tread. Foolish people act hastily, while wise people think before they act.

angry
When angry, count to a hundred. After counting to a hundred, your anger will have gone!

answer
A soft answer turneth away wrath. If someone is angry with you, don't show anger in return.

anything
If anything can go wrong, it will. Never assume that nothing will go wrong.

appearances
Appearances are deceptive. Never judge by appearances.

apple
An apple a day keeps the doctor away. Eating healthy food will keep you in good health.
The apple never falls far from the tree. Members of the same family are likely to retain family characteristics.
The apples on the far side of the wall are sweetest. Things which are difficult to get are always the most sought after.
The rotten apple injures its neighbours. A bad thing or person will affect those around it.

army
An army marches on its stomach. A well-fed soldier is likely to be the best fighter.

art
Art is long, life is short (Ars longa, vita brevis). 1. There is so much to learn in life, but only a short time in which to learn it. 2. Art lasts longer than the artist who created it.

ask
Ask no questions and you'll hear no lies. Don't show curiosity.

PROVERBS

ass
Every ass likes to hear himself bray. Fools like the sound of their own voices.

attack
Attack is the best form of defence. It is better to take the initiative than to wait for something to happen.

baby
Don't throw out the baby with the bathwater. In an effort to achieve your aim, don't overlook important details on the way.

back
His back is broad enough to bear blame. Describes a person who is strong enough to bear responsibility.
You scratch my back and I'll scratch yours. Help me out and I'll help you.

bad
A bad penny always comes back. Bad things always turn up again.
A bad workman always blames his tools. Describes a person who does a bad job, and blames everything but himself.

bake
As you bake, so shall you brew. This has a similar meaning to *As you make your bed, so shall you lie on it.*

bargain
A bargain's a bargain. You should stick by your agreements, no matter how things turn out.
Make the best of a bad bargain. If things go wrong and you can't change them, it's best to accept the situation.

barking
Barking dogs seldom bite. People who make the most noise are usually the ones who act least.

battle
The first blow is half the battle. The person who gets in first has the advantage.

be
Be what you would seem to be. Don't be a hypocrite.

bear
Bear and forbear. Be patient and tolerant.

beast
When the wind is in the east, 'tis neither good for man nor beast. Weather proverb: the east wind is generally a cold wind.

beat
If you can't beat them, join them. If what you suggest is totally opposed, join the majority.

PROVERBS

beauty
Beauty is but skin-deep. You can't judge things by their appearance alone.
Beauty is in the eye of the beholder. Judging appearance is up to the individual.
A thing of beauty is a joy for ever. Experience of something beautiful remains with you always.

bed
Go to bed with the lamb and rise with the lark. Early to bed and early to rise.
As you make your bed, so you must lie on it. You must accept the consequences of your own actions.

beggar
Set a beggar on horseback and he'll ride to the devil. Someone unused to riches may go badly wrong if wealth suddenly comes their way.

begin
It's good to begin well, but better to end well. Start a job well, but make sure that you see it through to the end.

beginning
Every beginning is hard. Starting something is always difficult.
Everything must have a beginning. Everyone has to start somewhere.

beginnings
From small beginnings come great things. Even the most important things start in a small way.

begins
He who begins many things, finishes but few. If you take on too many different jobs, you won't have time for them all.

believe
Believe not all that you see nor half what you hear. Nothing is ever quite what it seems.
We soon believe what we desire. Most people believe what they want to believe.

believing
Seeing is believing. You are likely to believe what you see with your own eyes.

bend
Better bend than break. Better to wait and consider, rather than be totally opposed to something.

best
The best of men are men at best. However admirable people may be, they are still only human.
The best things come in small packages. Things don't have to be large to be good.
The best things in life are free. This is a line from a popular song, written in 1927.

bigger
The bigger they are, the harder they fall. The more powerful and successful people are, the more they have to lose.

bird
A bird in hand is worth two in the bush. Hold on to what you have, rather than waiting for something better.
The early bird catches the worm. Act quickly and in good time.

PROVERBS

Birds of a feather flock together. People are likely to be happier in the company of those with like minds.

bite
If you can't bite, never show your teeth. Don't start trouble if you can't defend yourself.

biter
The biter is sometimes bit. The tables are sometimes turned so that the attacker becomes the victim.

bitten
Once bitten, twice shy. A bad experience makes you want to avoid a second one.

blarney
Kiss the Blarney Stone. Anyone who kisses the Blarney Stone near Cork, Ireland, is said to have the ability to persuade or charm.

blind
If the blind lead the blind, both shall fall into the ditch. Those without knowledge should not try to lead or teach others.
In the country of the blind, the one-eyed man is king. When people around you are ignorant, even a little knowledge will give you an advantage.
None so blind as those that won't see. It's pointless trying to convince someone who is totally prejudiced.

blood
You can't get blood out of a stone. You can't get something from someone too mean to give it.

books
Books and friends should be few but good. If you have too many of each, you will have little time to enjoy them.

borrower
Neither a borrower nor a lender be. Borrowing and lending money or possessions can lead to trouble between friends; so it is better not to do either.

borrowing
He that goes a-borrowing goes a-sorrowing. Anything borrowed, especially money, has to be paid back, and the sorrow comes when there's no money left to pay the debt.

bough
Don't cut off the bough you're standing on. Don't get rid of your only support.

branch
The highest branch is not the safest roost. Those at the top have the farthest to fall.

brass
Where there's muck there's brass (or luck). Dirty work can be the most rewarding.

PROVERBS

bread
Bread is the staff of life. You cannot exist without food.

breakfast
If you sing before breakfast, you'll cry before night. Happiness never lasts long.

brevity
Brevity is the soul of wit. A short answer is often the most eloquent.

broth
Too many cooks spoil the broth. Something can be ruined if too many people try to do the same job at the same time.

bull
Take the bull by the horns. Cope with a problem without fear.

bully
A bully is always a coward. Bullies always choose victims among those smaller or weaker than themselves.

burn
Burn not your house to fright the mouse away. Don't go to extremes to solve a simple problem.

butterfly
Break a butterfly on a wheel. Don't use more force than is really needed.

bygones
Let bygones be bygones. Forget past quarrels and forgive.

cake
You can't have your cake and eat it. You must make a decision and stick to it.

candle
Light not a candle to the sun. Don't try to describe the obvious.

cap
If the cap fits, wear it. If the description applies to you, accept it and be warned.

care
Care will kill a cat. Worrying won't help a problem.
'Don't care' was made to care. Those who are careless will discover the folly of their ways.

PROBERBS

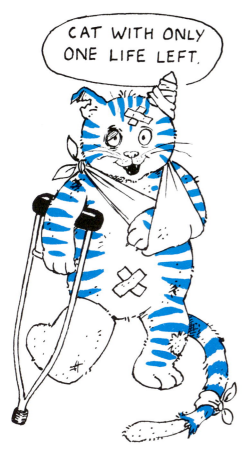

cat
A cat has nine lives. A cat seems to escape danger more than other animals.
Like a cat on hot bricks. Describes a worried and nervous person.
When the cat's away, the mice will play. When the person in charge is absent, people will do as they please.
There are more ways of killing a cat than by choking it with cream. There are more ways than one of getting something done.

catch
Catch as catch can. Get all you can in the ways you know best.

chain
The chain is no stronger than its weakest link. If one part of the chain breaks, then the whole chain is completely useless.

change
There is nothing permanent except change. The only unchanging aspect of life is change.
A change is as good as a rest. A change of scene is often as effective as a holiday.

charity
Charity begins at home. The meaning of this has changed. It once meant that although charity began at home, it did not end there. Now it tends to mean 'you may need help, but I must help myself first'.
Charity covers a multitude of sins. Originally this read 'Charity shall cover the multitude of sins'. It means, you should be forgiving to those who sin.

chatters
Who chatters to you will chatter of you. If someone gossips freely to you, they will most likely gossip about you.

cheap
Ill ware is never cheap. A useless bargain will cost you more in the end.

cheat
He that will cheat at play will cheat you anyway. Anyone who cheats at a game will be a cheat in other ways.
Cheats never prosper. Deceit will not help you.

cheerful
A cheerful look makes a dish a feast. A happy face can turn something ordinary into something special.

chickens
Don't count your chickens before they're hatched. Don't assume you have gained something until it has been proved.

child
A burned child dreads the fire. A harsh experience is not easily forgotten.

PROVERBS

SEEN BUT NOT HEARD

children
Little children should be seen and not heard. Children should be silent and not speak until they are spoken to.
Children and chicken must be always picking. Children are always hungry.

circumstances
Circumstances alter cases. If the conditions change, then the original agreement is no longer valid.

cleanliness
Cleanliness is next to godliness. A clean person is likely to be a moral person.

clothes
Clothes don't make the man. It is the person that matters, not the clothes they wear.

cloud
Every cloud has a silver lining. However unpleasant things are, something good will come out of them.

clouds
If there were no clouds, we should not enjoy the sun. If the sun shone all the time, you would not appreciate it.

coat
Cut your coat according to your cloth. Judge how much to spend by the amount you have available.

company
A man is known by the company he keeps. The world will judge you by those with whom you associate.

comparisons
Comparisons are odious. You should not make judgments between two people, since they will almost certainly be unjust.

contented
A contented mind is a perpetual feast. A contented mind gives lasting happiness.

cow
You can't sell the cow and drink the milk. You can't have it both ways: either you enjoy what you have or you sell it.

crab
You cannot make a crab walk straight. Don't attempt to do the impossible.

cradle
The hand that rocks the cradle rules the world. A mother's influence is one of the greatest of all.

credit
Give credit where credit is due. Praise should be given when it is deserved.

crown
Uneasy lies the head that wears a crown. Being a leader is not simple or safe.

crutches
One foot is better than two crutches. It is better to accept what you have, little though it be, than to risk something worse.

PROVERBS

cry
Don't cry before you're hurt. Don't anticipate injury – it may not happen.

cup
There's many a slip 'twixt cup and lip. Until you actually have something in your possession, you can't be sure of it.

cured
What can't be cured must be endured. If nothing can be done to help the situation, then you must put up with it.

curiosity
Curiosity killed the cat. Being curious can lead you into trouble.

curses
Curses, like chickens, come home to roost. Those who threaten others may find they bring trouble upon themselves.

custom
Custom without reason is but ancient error. Because something has always been done, it should not be assumed that it is good practice.

darkest
The darkest hour is just before the dawn. Things may seem bad, but they will almost certainly improve.

dead
Dead men tell no tales. Once someone is dead they remain silent for ever.
He goes long barefoot that waits for a dead man's shoes. A warning about the folly of waiting for someone to die simply to gain their possessions.
Always speak well of the dead. Since they cannot answer for themselves, it is up to those remaining to speak well of them.

deaf
None is so deaf as those who won't hear. It is pointless trying to make someone listen who is determined not to.

51

PROVERBS

death
Death is a great leveller. Death treats all people equally, no matter how important they were in life.

debt
Out of debt, out of danger. Owing money is worrying and settling a debt gives peace of mind.

deceives
If a man deceives me once, shame on him; if he deceives me twice, shame on me. If you have experienced deceit once, you would be foolish to allow it again.
He that once deceives is ever suspected. If you behave deceitfully, you will not be trusted again.

deeds
Deeds, not words. You are judged by what you do, rather than what you say.

despair
Despair gives courage to a coward. When there is no hope at all, even a coward has nothing to lose.

devil
Better the devil you know than the devil you don't. Something unknown is more frightening than something already experienced.
Every man for himself, and the devil take the hindmost. Look after yourself first and leave others to look after themselves.
He that sups with the devil must have a long spoon. If you having dealings with someone untrustworthy you must be very cautious.
The devil finds work for idle hands. Those who have nothing to do will end up by doing something wrong.
Give the devil his due. Assess someone fairly, even if they are not liked.

diamond
Diamond cut diamond. It takes someone of great strength to match another strong person.

die
Never say die. Never give up hope.

difficult
What is difficult is done at once; the impossible takes a little longer. Nothing is impossible.

dirt
Fling dirt enough and some will stick. If you tell enough unpleasant tales about someone, some of them will be believed.
Every man must eat a peck of dirt before he dies. No-one goes through life without some hurt or harm.

PROVERBS

discretion
Discretion is the better part of valour. What appears to be cowardice may, in fact, be wise caution.

disease
The remedy may be worse than the disease. Don't be too hasty to correct what appears to be wrong. The remedy may cause more harm.

diseases
Desperate diseases call for desperate remedies. If you are in real trouble, a desperate decision might seem to be the only way out.

dish
No dish pleases all palates alike. Not everyone likes the same things.

distance
Distance lends enchantment to the view. Seen from a long way off, things may seem better than they really are.

do
Do as I say, not as I do. Never mind how I behave, do as I tell you.
Do as you would be done by. Behave to others as you would want them to treat you.

dog
Better to be the head of a dog than the tail of a lion. Better to be top of a small group than bottom of a large one.
Why keep a dog and bark yourself? If you have someone to do a job for you, there is no point in doing it yourself.
Dog does not eat dog. Those in crime do not give each other away.
Help a lame dog over a stile. Help someone in difficulties.
Love me, love my dog. Anyone who wants to be my friend must accept me as I am, with all my failings.
You can't teach an old dog new tricks. It's difficult for old people to learn new skills.
Give a dog a bad name and hang him. Once someone's reputation has been damaged they cannot retrieve it.

dogs
Two dogs strive for a bone and a third runs away with it. If you get into a dispute with someone, beware that a third person doesn't take advantage of your quarrel.
All are not thieves that dogs bark at. Don't judge by appearances.

door
A golden key opens every door. Money will give you an entrance anywhere.
If one door shuts, another opens. If you fail, try again; there will be other opportunities.

doubt
When in doubt, do nowt. When you're not sure, take no action.

PROVERBS

ear
You can't make a silk purse out of a sow's ear. You can't make something of good quality from poor materials.

easy
Easy come, easy go. What was easily won is easily lost.
It's easy to be wise after the event. Once you know the outcome, it's a simple matter to suggest how things could have been done.

eggs
Don't teach your grandmother to suck eggs. Don't try to tell more experienced people how to do their jobs.
You can't make an omelette without breaking eggs. It's impossible to do anything without sacrificing something.
He that would have eggs must endure the cackling of hens. If you want something, you must be prepared to put up with some discomfort.

empty
Empty vessels make the most sound. Foolish people are also the noisiest.

end
All good things must come to an end. Nothing pleasant goes on for ever.
The end justifies the means. If the result is good, it doesn't matter what methods were used to achieve it.

envied
Better be envied than pitied. People who are envied are looked up to; those who are pitied are looked down upon.

err
To err is human. Everyone makes mistakes.

events
Coming events cast their shadows before. You usually get some idea of what is going to happen by clues in advance.

everything
Everything comes to him that waits. Someone who waits patiently will usually get what they want in the end.
A place for everything and everything in its place. Life is simpler and easier if you are tidy and methodical.

evils
Choose the lesser of two evils. If you have to choose between two bad choices, choose the least bad.

excuse
A bad excuse is better than none. This is said to those who offer a poor excuse.

expects
Blessed is he who expects nothing, for he shall never be disappointed. If you expect little from life, any pleasant surprise is a bonus.

experience
Experience is the mother of wisdom. As you learn, both by your mistakes and successes, you gain wisdom.

eye
The eye is bigger than the belly. This refers to someone who helps themselves to more food than they can really eat.
An eye for an eye, a tooth for a tooth. This refers to revenge, getting exact justice for crimes committed.
What the eye doesn't see, the heart doesn't grieve over. Things that happen without your knowledge, especially unpleasant ones, do not worry you.

PROVERBS

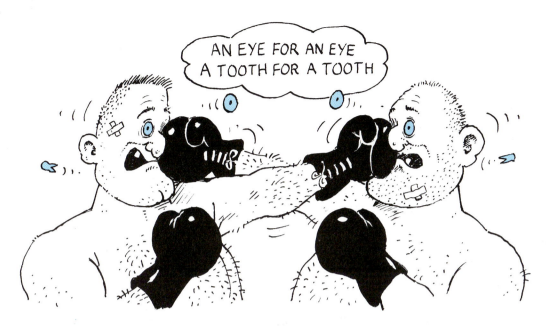

familiarity
Familiarity breeds contempt. The more familiar you are with a person or thing, the less respect you have.

father
Like father, like son. A child often behaves like its parents.
He whose father is judge, goes safe to his trial. Parents cannot judge their own children fairly.

feast
A contented mind is a perpetual feast. If you are contented, then you will enjoy peace of mind and happiness.

feathers
Fine feathers make fine birds. Said of people who dress well to impress others.

fiddle
There's many a good tune played on an old fiddle. Older people can be just as useful as young ones.

fight
He that fights and runs away may live to fight another day. Don't be foolhardy; save yourself for another battle.

finders
Finders keepers. Someone who finds something should be allowed to keep it.

first
First come, first served. The first to arrive will be the first to receive attention.

fish
That fish will soon be caught that nibbles at every bait. Curiosity and inquisitiveness will lead to your downfall.
The best fish swim near the bottom. The best things are the most difficult to obtain.
There are as good fish in the sea as ever came out of it. Things may have gone wrong this time, but another opportunity will come.

flatterer
When the flatterer pipes, then the devil dances. Flattery does not bring good, either to the flatterer or the person being flattered.

PROVERBS

fool
Better to be a fool than a knave. Better to be innocent and foolish than guilty.
A fool and his money are soon parted. Don't be persuaded to spend money on things you don't really want or need.
There's no fool like an old fool. An elderly and experienced person can seem more foolish than a young one.

fools
Young men think old men fools, and old men know young men to be so. The enthusiasm of the young and the wisdom of the old never mix.

foot
Never tell your enemy that your foot aches. Don't expose your weaknesses to someone who can wield power over you.

footprints
Footprints in the sands of time are not made by sitting down. People who have made their mark on the world have been active in what they do.

forbidden
Forbidden fruit is sweetest. Something that is forbidden always seems more desirable and exciting.

forelock
Take time by the forelock. Take advantage of the present, the past cannot be changed.

forewarned
Forewarned is forearmed. Knowing about future danger helps you to cope with it when it arrives.

forgive
Forgive and forget. Don't harbour feelings of revenge; put such thoughts from your mind.

fortune
Fortune favours the bold. People who act bravely deserve, and find, good luck.
Fortune knocks at least once at every man's gate. When an opportunity comes, seize it.

friend
A friend in need is a friend indeed. Someone who helps you when you are in trouble is a true friend.

friends
The best of friends must part. However pleasant, all relationships must come to an end.
May God defend me from my friends; I can defend myself from my enemies. A misguided friend can do far more damage than an enemy.

PROVERBS

IT'S BETTER TO GIVE THAN TO RECEIVE

gate
A creaking gate hangs long. Those who are not in good health often last longest.

give
It's better to give than receive. It's better to be generous than to take from others.

gluttony
Gluttony kills more than the sword. Overeating is dangerous and can kill.

gnats
Men strain at gnats and swallow camels. Some people concern themselves with small wrongs and overlook large ones.

God
God helps those who help themselves. Don't expect to get something without working for it first.
You cannot serve God and mammon. You must choose between holy and worldly things.
All things are possible with God. With God's help you can do anything.

gods
The mills of the gods grind slowly, but they grind exceedingly small. Rewards and punishments may not come immediately, but they will come in the end.

gold
All that glitters is not gold. What looks attractive at first may prove to be worthless.
When we have gold we are in fear, when we have none we are in danger. If someone is rich, they are afraid of thieves; if someone is poor they have no means of support.

goose
Don't kill the goose that lays the golden eggs. Don't cut off the source of your success or profit.
What's sauce for the goose is sauce for the gander. What's good for one person is good for another; you can't complain if you are treated equally.
He that has a goose will get a goose. The rich continue to get richer.

grasp
Grasp all, lose all. Don't be greedy, or you may lose what you already have.

PROVERBS

grass
The grass is always greener on the other side of the fence. Discontent with what you have leads you to believe that others are more fortunate.

Greek
When Greek meets Greek, then comes the tug of war. When two equally-matched opponents meet, it becomes a real struggle.

ground
He that lies upon the ground can fall no lower. One compensation for being at the bottom of the ladder is that you can't fall any lower.

growing
A growing youth has a wolf in his belly. The young are always hungry.

guest
A constant guest is never welcome. A too-frequent visitor can earn the dislike of his or her friends.

hands
Many hands make light work. If the task is shared by many, then it will be easier.

handsome
Handsome is as handsome does. The character of a person should be decided by their actions, not by their appearance.

hare
First catch your hare. Wait till you've got what you need before you decide what to do with it.
You can't run with the hare and hunt with the hounds. You can't be friendly with two opposing types of people.

hares
If you run after two hares, you'll catch neither. Don't do two things at once.

haste
Make haste slowly. Think carefully before you rush into something; give it time and thought.
Haste trips over its own heels or *More haste, less speed.* When you try to do something in a hurry it often takes longer due to carelessness.

hasty
A hasty man drinks his tea with a fork. Another version of the 'haste' proverbs.

hay
Make hay while the sun shines. Take advantage of something while it is available.

MANY HANDS MAKE LIGHT WORK

PROVERBS

head
You can't put an old head on young shoulders. You can't expect a young person to have the judgment of someone older and more experienced.

heads
Two heads are better than one. In a difficulty it's better to seek advice rather than carrying on alone.

health
Health is better than wealth. It's better to be healthy than rich.

heart
It's a sad heart that never rejoices. No-one should be sad or miserable all the time.

hearts
Kind hearts are more than coronets. It's your character that matters, not your social standing.

heat
If you don't like the heat, get out of the kitchen. If the pace is too fast for you, then step aside and allow others more capable to take over.

hedge
A hedge between keeps friendship green. or *Love your neighbour, yet pull not down your hedge.* People are likely to be better friends when they don't see too much of each other.

heels
One pair of heels is often worth two pairs of hands. When the odds are against you, it's better to run than to stand and fight.

hell
The road to hell is paved with good intentions. Good intentions aren't enough; deeds are what count.

help
A little help is worth a deal of pity. It's better to give real help to someone rather than offer them sympathy.

hesitates
He who hesitates is lost. Anyone who delays will lose their chance of success.

history
History repeats itself. If it has happened once, it will happen again.

hog
What can you expect from a hog but a grunt? If an ill-mannered person is rude to you, it's only what you should expect.

home
East or west, home's best, or *There's no place like home.* Home is the best place to be.

honesty
Honesty is the best policy. You will always gain the trust of people by being honest.

hook
The bait hides the hook. An attractive bargain may have a hidden flaw.

PROVERBS

hope
If it were not for hope, the heart would break. Everyone needs hope to recover from their troubles and griefs.
Hope for the best, but prepare for the worst. Optimism is fine, but always be cautious.
Hope springs eternal in the human breast. People are always hoping.

horse
It's useless flogging a dead horse. It's no use trying to get satisfaction from something which cannot provide it.
You can lead a horse to water, but you can't make him drink. You can't force someone to do something they don't want to do.
Don't look a gift horse in the mouth. Don't criticize something which has been freely given to you.
All lay loads on a willing horse. Anyone who is willing and good-natured is likely to be asked to do more than others.
Every horse thinks its own pack is heaviest. Everyone believes that they are doing the most work.

houses
People who live in glass houses shouldn't throw stones. People with faults of their own should not complain of faults in others.

hunger
Hunger is the best sauce. If you're really hungry, you need no sauce to give you an appetite.

ignorance
Where ignorance is bliss, 'tis folly to be wise. If you are happy not knowing something, then it is better that way.

imitation
Imitation is the sincerest form of flattery. If you copy someone's ideas or ways, then you obviously admire that person.

impressions
First impressions are the most rewarding. The feelings you have about someone at the first meeting are likely to stay with you.

inspiration
Ninety per cent of inspiration is perspiration. Most good ideas don't come easily, but from hard work.

PROVERBS

Jack
A Jack of all trades is master of none. Someone who tries their hand at too many things will never be expert in any.

jam
Jam tomorrow and jam yesterday; but never jam today. People remember the good things of yesterday and look forward to the future, but never appreciate the good things of the moment.

jest
There's many a true word spoken in jest. Even though a remark is made as a joke, it often contains an element of truth.

joy
Sudden joy kills sooner than excessive grief. Sudden great excitement is more likely to kill than long grief.

just
A just war is better than an unjust peace. It is better to fight for a fair world than live in an unfair one.

kindness
Kindness comes of will. Kindness cannot be obtained by force.

knowledge
Doubt is the key of knowledge. Curiosity will lead you to learn more.

labourer
The labourer is worthy of his hire. Anyone who does an honest job deserves to be paid adequately.

ladder
He who would climb the ladder must begin at the bottom. Whoever starts at the bottom will learn all there is to know as they rise to the top.

late
Better late than never. It's better to arrive late than not at all.

PROVERBS

laugh
Laugh and the world laughs with you; weep and you weep alone. Everyone wants to share the joy of a cheerful person, but they shun someone who is miserable.

lazy
Lazy people take the most pains. Those who take short cuts in their work will have to do it again, and so end up doing more work.

leap
Look before you leap. Think carefully before you act.

learn
Never too old to learn. No-one is so old that they can't usefully learn new things.

learning
A little learning is a dangerous thing. Those who know only a little can deceive themselves into believing they know all.

leisure
Idle people have the least leisure. If you are idle all the time you cannot know the pleasure of leisure.

lend
Lend and lose the loan, or gain an enemy. If you lend something you must expect to lose it, or to offend by asking for it back.

leopard
The leopard can't change its spots. People's characters remain the same, no matter how much else changes.

liar
A liar is not believed when he tells the truth. If you lie, people will assume that everything you say is untrue.

liars
Liars should have good memories. Liars frequently forget what they have lied about, and so give themselves away by telling a different lie.

liberty
Lean liberty is better than fat slavery. It is better to be free and without riches than rich and enslaved.

lie
One lie makes many. If you tell one lie, you'll often have to tell many more to support it.

life
Where there's life, there's hope. As long as you are alive there is always something to look forward to.
Life is short and time is swift. Make the most of life.

PROVERBS

lightning
Lightning never strikes twice in the same place. The same unusual happenings and events do not occur more than once to the same person.

listeners
Listeners never hear any good of themselves. If you eavesdrop on a conversation, the chances are you'll hear criticism of yourself.

live
Live not to eat, but eat to live. Gluttony is not to be recommended, you should eat only as much as is necessary for life.

love
The course of true love never did run smooth. Those in love will encounter problems on the way.
All's fair in love and war. When strong emotions are involved, you cannot have any real rules.
It is love that makes the world go round. Love is so necessary to people that it seems to move the Earth and the Sun.
Love is blind. Those in love cannot see faults in their partners.

lucky
It's better to be born lucky than rich. If you're rich you only have money; if you're lucky you may have other gifts which money can't buy.

lump
If you don't like it, you can lump it. Whether you like it or not, you have to put up with it.

marry
Marry in haste and repent at leisure. If two people marry without due consideration, it is likely to be unsuccessful.

masters
No man can serve two masters. You can't be totally loyal to two people or two ideas at the same time.

meat
One man's meat is another man's poison. The fact that one person enjoys something doesn't mean that everyone else will.

mend
It's never too late to mend. It's never too late to change your ways for the better.

minds
Little things please little minds. People of small intellect are happy doing simple things.
Great minds think alike. Wise people tend to come to the same conclusions.

PROVERBS

misfortunes
Misfortunes never come singly. One mishap is often followed by another.
Our worst misfortunes are those which never happen. The calamities that we worry about most are the ones that tend not to happen.

miss
A miss is as good as a mile. If you fail in a small way, you might just as well have failed in a big way.

mistakes
He who makes no mistakes makes nothing. If you are so careful that you never make a mistake, you aren't likely to achieve very much.
Wise men learn by other men's mistakes; fools by their own. If you observe the mistakes of others you are unlikely to repeat them yourself.

money
The love of money is the root of all evil. Almost all of the world's evils are caused by greed.
Lend your money and lose a friend. Friendships are broken when you ask for a debt to be repaid.
Money is a good servant, but a bad master. Don't let money be your god, but use it well.

mountain
If the mountain will not come to Muhammad, Muhammad must go to the mountain. If whatever is needed cannot or will not come to a person, then that person must go and find it for themselves.

mouse
Don't make yourself a mouse, or the cat will eat you. Don't make yourself look small, or bullies will take advantage of you.

mouths
Out of the mouths of babes and sucklings. Wise remarks coming from the very young.

name
A good name is sooner lost than won. It takes time to earn a good name. If it is lost, it is lost for ever.
A man lives a generation; a name to the end of all generations. A family name does not die out but is passed on through the generations.

naughty
Naughty boys sometimes make good men. Those who were badly behaved in their youth often become well-respected in their adulthood.

PROVERBS

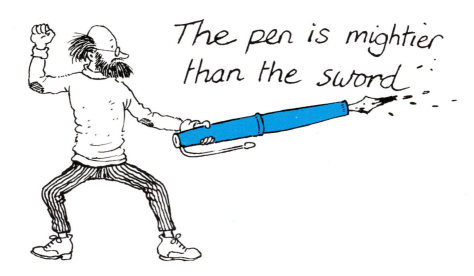

necessity
Necessity is the mother of invention. When you are faced with a difficult problem, you will often think of an ingenious way out.

news
Bad news travels fast. Bad news reaches you more quickly than good news.
No news is good news. News can be good or bad; the fact that there is no news means that all could be well.

nothing
Nothing venture, nothing gain. If you try nothing, you will gain nothing.

numbers
There's safety in numbers. If many other people are doing or thinking as you do, then you are probably safer.

oaks
Many strokes fell tall oaks. A big task can be completed by long and patient work.

obey
He that cannot obey, cannot command. If you are unable to obey orders, then you're unlikely to be able to give them yourself.

one
One thing at a time, and that done well, is a very good thing, as many can tell. Don't try to do too many things at once, but do one task well.

pains
No pains, no gains. You won't gain anything without some trouble.

parsnips
Fine words butter no parsnips. Fine talk is all very well, but it doesn't produce results.

pen
The pen is mightier than the sword. What is written can often have more power than brute force.

PROVERBS

pence
Take care of the pence and the pounds will look after themselves. If you take care of the small details, the rest will fall into place.

penny
In for a penny, in for a pound. If you have decided to take part in something, you might just as well do it wholeheartedly.
A penny for your thoughts? What are you thinking about?

pin
He that will not stoop for a pin shall never be worth a pound. If you don't consider small profits, you will never be rich.

pint
You can't get a pint into a quart pot. You can't do the impossible.

piper
He who pays the piper calls the tune. If you are paying for something you are entitled to say how it is to be done.

pot
A watched pot never boils. Worrying about a situation will not help.

praise
Praise makes good men better and bad men worse. Good people are able to accept praise, but bad ones allow it to go to their heads.

present
There's no time like the present. If something needs to be done, then it should be done now.

prevention
Prevention is better than cure. It's always better to stop something from happening rather than to put it right after it has taken place.

price
Every man has his price. Anyone can be persuaded to do something by the offer of a bribe.

pride
Pride goes before a fall. A proud person is likely to fall into trouble.

procrastination
Procrastination is the thief of time. Do what needs to be done quickly; to delay simply wastes time.

purse
He that has a full purse never needed a friend. The well-off are rarely short of friends.
A heavy purse makes a light heart. Those with enough money can afford to be happy.

quarrel
It takes two to make a quarrel. There are two sides to every argument.

questions
Ask no questions and you'll be told no lies. Said to those who persist in asking awkward questions.

race
Slow but sure wins the race. Those who hurry may stumble; those who take care will win.

rains
It never rains but it pours. When disaster comes, it comes in plenty.

PROVERBS

rats
Rats desert a sinking ship. Disloyal and untrustworthy people are the first to disappear if you are in trouble.

receiver
The receiver is as bad as the thief. Whoever deals in stolen goods is as guilty as the thief himself.

rod
Spare the rod and spoil the child. If punishment is not meted out to a bad child, he or she will suffer in the long run.

rose
A rose by any other name would smell as sweet. It doesn't matter what something is called; it's the thing itself that is important.
No rose without a thorn. Nothing is ever perfect.

rosebuds
Gather ye rosebuds while ye may. Take what pleasures you can now; you may not be able to do so later.

roundabouts
What you lose on the swings you gain on the roundabouts. What you lose on one thing, you gain on another.

sands
The sands of time are running out. There is not much time left.

scholars
The greatest scholars are not always the wisest men. Being learned doesn't make you wise in all things.

seeing
Seeing is believing. You have to accept the evidence of your own eyes.

self
Self-preservation is the first law of nature. Look after yourself first.

seven
Rain before seven, fine before eleven. A weather proverb: early showers often clear to give a fine day.

shadow
Catch not the shadow and lose the substance. Don't get so involved with the detail of something that you miss the main point.

PROVERBS

sheep
There's a black sheep in every flock. Every family (or group of people) has its rogue.
You might as well be hanged for a sheep as a lamb. If you are going to do something wrong, you might just as well commit a greater crime as a smaller one.

ship
It's no use spoiling the ship for a ha'porth of tar. If a job's worth doing, it's worth doing well.

sight
Out of sight, out of mind. If something is not seen, it is soon forgotten.

silence
Speech is silver, silence is golden. Sometimes it is better and more eloquent to remain silent.

sins
The sins of the fathers are visited upon the children. People are punished for the misdeeds of their forebears.

sky
A red sky at night is the shepherd's delight. A red sky in the morning is the shepherd's warning. A weather proverb, warning of fine weather, or rain.

sow
As you sow, so shall you reap. Your eventual reward will be based on how you lived your life.

speak
Speak well of your friend, of your enemy say nothing. If you can't say something good, say nothing.

speaks
He that speaks well, fights well. The person who is honest can be trusted to fight alongside you.

spirit
The spirit is willing, but the flesh is weak. However much you wish to do something, you may find yourself incapable of doing it.

sprat
To throw out a sprat to catch a mackerel. To sacrifice something of small importance in order to achieve something much bigger.

spur
Never spur a willing horse. Don't try to make a willing person do more than they can. They may end up by doing less.

step
Step after step the ladder is ascended. Persevere and, sooner or later, you will achieve your aim.

sticks
Sticks and stones may break my bones, but words will never hurt me. Jeering at me won't do any harm.

stitch
A stitch in time saves nine. Take action now, and save a greater problem later.

PROVERBS

stone
Cast not the first stone. Before you criticize others, make sure you are not guilty yourself.
A rolling stone gathers no moss. Someone who frequently moves from place to place will not pick up habits and ways, good or bad.

straw
The last straw breaks the camel's back. This is said when a point is reached beyond which patience and endurance cannot go.
A drowning man will clutch at a straw. When all else has failed, people in a desperate situation will turn to anything which offers the slightest hope.

sublime
From the sublime to the ridiculous is but a step. Sometimes it doesn't require a large change to move from a serious situation to a laughable one.

success
Nothing succeeds like success. Once you succeed, you gain confidence to move on to even greater successes.

sundial
What's the good of a sundial in the shade? If you have talent, then don't hide it from the world.

sure
Better to be sure than sorry. It's better to choose a safe path than take a dangerous one unnecessarily.

swallow
One swallow doesn't make a summer. Because something pleasant has taken place doesn't mean that things in general have improved.

sweep
If each would sweep before his own door, we should have a clean city. If every individual did something to help, then life would be better for everyone.

tale
A good tale is none the worse for being told twice. People are prepared to hear an interesting story more than once.

thorn
I'll not pull the thorn out of your foot and put it in my own. I will help you, but not if it injures me.

tiger
Who rides a tiger is afraid to dismount. If you're doing something wrong, it's hard to stop, in case you are found out.

PROVERBS

time
Time is the great healer. Grief and misery will heal in time.
Time and tide wait for no man. If you have something important to do, see that it is done immediately.
An inch of gold will not buy an inch of time. Nothing can buy back wasted time.
For the busy man time passes quickly. Time doesn't hang heavy for those with plenty to do.

tomorrow
Never put off till tomorrow what may be done today. If something needs to be done, don't delay by putting it off until another day.
Here today and gone tomorrow. Some things last for only a short time.

tongue
A still tongue makes a wise head. If you talk too much, you are liable to miss words of wisdom from others.

tooth
The tongue ever turns to the aching tooth. When something worries you, you are likely to keep thinking about it.

tortoise
The tortoise wins the race while the hare is sleeping. From one of *Aesop's Fables*. Slow and sure will win in the end.

travel
It is better to travel hopefully than to arrive. If you are working towards a goal, the work itself is often more rewarding than the completion.

trouble
Don't meet trouble half-way. Don't worry about something before it actually happens.
A trouble shared is a trouble halved. If you confide in someone about misfortune, it is easier to bear.

trust
Put your trust in God, but keep your powder dry. Trust in God, but nevertheless take every precaution yourself.

truth
Speak the truth and shame the devil. However much you are tempted to lie, it is always better to speak the truth.
Truth is stranger than fiction. Things in real life can often be much odder than something invented.

turn
One good turn deserves another. If someone helps you, try to help them in return.

unexpected
Nothing is so certain as the unexpected. It is certain that things which are unexpected will surprise you.

united
United we stand, divided we fall. If people work together, they have a stronger chance of winning through.

variety
Variety is the spice of life. People get bored with the same old things; something new arouses their interest.

virtue
Virtue is its own reward. You should never expect to be rewarded for a good deed. The satisfaction you get from doing it should be enough.

volunteer
One volunteer is worth two pressed men. Those who are compelled to do something are much less likely to do the job well than someone who is willing.

wagon
Hitch your wagon to a star. Always aim high.
When the wagon of fortune goes well, spite and envy hang onto the wheels. Good luck will always cause jealousy in others.

walk
Learn to walk before you run. Take things in easy stages, and learn as you go along.

walls
Walls have ears. Don't speak too freely; you may be overheard.
Men, not walls, make a city safe. Wise government, not armed might, is the best protection of a country.

waste
Waste not, want not. If you're careful with what you have, you'll not go hungry.

waters
Still waters run deep. Quiet people are often the deepest thinkers.

way
Better to ask the way than go astray. If you are unsure about something, it is better to take advice.

wear
It's better to wear out than rust out. It's better to be active than idle.

wheel
The worst wheel on the cart creaks most. The most inefficient person is the one who makes most complaints.

will
Where there's a will, there's a way. If you are determined to do something, you will find a way of doing it.
Will is no skill. Wanting to do something is not the same as being able to do it.

wind
It's an ill wind that blows nobody any good. Somebody, somewhere is able to profit from misfortune.

wish
The wish is father to the thought. If you wish something were true, you can sometimes believe that it really is so.

wishes
If wishes were horses, beggars would ride. If all we needed was to wish for something, then we could all be rich.

wolf
When the wolf comes in at the door, love flies out of the window. If people fall on hard times even love finds it difficult to survive.

words
A man of words and not of deeds is like a garden full of weeds. This describes someone who talks all the time rather than taking action.

PROBVERBS

worm
Even a worm will turn. Even the mildest of people will react if pushed too far.

worse
Worse things happen at sea. It could have been worse!

wound
Though the wound be healed, yet a scar remains. People do not forget the pain of old hurts and the lesson learned from them.

wrath
Let not the sun go down on your wrath. If you have an argument or quarrel, make every effort to settle it amicably before the day ends.

wrong
If anything can go wrong, it will. Even the best-laid plans can go awry.

wrongs
Two wrongs don't make a right. If someone does you a wrong, then having your revenge will not make things right.

yesterday
It's too late to call back yesterday. What has passed is gone and cannot be recaptured.

young
You're only young once. Take advantage of your youth while you have it.

yourself
Yourself first, others afterwards. Put your own self-interests before the good of others.

youth
Youth and age will not agree. The younger generation will never agree with the older one.

IDIOMS

IDIOMS

Idioms are phrases and expressions which are in common use. Most are very familiar, some are amusing, but the majority are not to be taken literally. If you say, 'My heart sank', you do not mean that your heart actually sank, but that you felt depressed because something had gone wrong. 'An itching palm' isn't really itchy. The expression describes someone who is greedy for money. In the following list, each entry is shown with a keyword and the idiom or phrase follows.

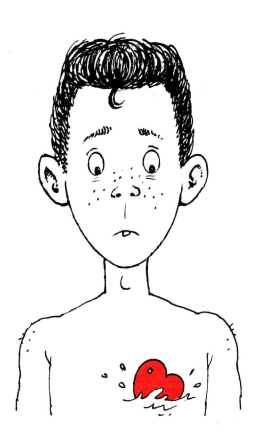

above
above all: especially, most importantly.
above board: openly, honestly, straightforward.
to be above yourself: to be conceited and act in a proud way.

accidents
a chapter of accidents: a series of misfortunes.

accord
of your own accord: without persuasion.

account
to take into account: to allow for, pay attention to.

accounts
by all accounts: according to the information available.

ace
to have an ace up your sleeve: to have a secret idea held in reserve.
within an ace of: close to achieving or doing something.

acid
the acid test: a very severe test to prove something beyond doubt.

across
to get something across: to make something understood.

act
to get caught in the act: to discover someone doing something questionable.
to get in on the act: to join someone in a successful venture.
to put on an act: to behave falsely, to conceal your true feelings.

action
out of action: not working, not in operation.

actions
actions speak louder than words: you are judged more by what you do than by what you say.

IDIOMS

Adam
Adam's ale: water.
not know from Adam: to be unacquainted with someone.

advantage
to take advantage of: to use for your own purposes, make good use of.

against
to be up against it: to be in severe trouble.

air
out of thin air: from nowhere, from nothing.

airs
give yourself airs: to be conceited or arrogant.

alive
alive and kicking: alert and active.

all
all in all: when all is considered.
all there: clever, able, bright.

all right
I'm all right, Jack: I'm doing very well (this implies that the speaker is only concerned with him or herself).

alley
a blind alley: a situation or act which leads nowhere.

allowance
make allowance for: to take into consideration.

alone
to go it alone: to do something without any help.

angel
an angel of mercy: someone who helps in a desperate situation.

angels
on the side of the angels: holding the correct moral view.

appearances
to keep up appearances: to continue to behave in a certain way to impress others.

apple
the apple of someone's eye: someone most dear to a person.

apple-cart
to upset the apple-cart: to spoil something which had been planned.

apple-pie
in apple-pie order: everything correct and in place.

Arab
street Arab: a waif or homeless city child.

ark
out of the ark: very old or old-fashioned.

arm
at arm's length: far away, at a certain distance.
to chance your arm: to take a risk.

IDIOMS

ashes
to rise from the ashes: to build something from destruction.

axe
to have an axe to grind: to have a personal or profitable interest in something.

babe
a babe in arms: someone not very experienced.

baby
to be left holding the baby: to be left to take care of something difficult.

back
to get someone's back up: to annoy someone.
to get your own back: to have your revenge.
to have your back to the wall: to be forced into a defensive position.
to put your back into something: to do something with great enthusiasm and effort.

backwards
to know something backwards: to know something very well.

bad
to go from bad to worse: to become worse than before.
not bad: actually quite good.

bag
a bag of tricks: tools or items needed for a special purpose.
it's in the bag: it's certain or sure.

baker
a baker's dozen: thirteen.

balance
in the balance: touch and go, something not yet decided.

ball
the ball's in your court: it's your responsibility, it's your turn to make a decision.
to keep the ball rolling: to keep a discussion or activity going.
to play ball with: to work with someone, co-operate.

balloon
when the balloon goes up: when something serious occurs.

bananas
to go bananas: to go wild or angry.

IDIOMS

bargepole
I wouldn't touch it with a bargepole: I would avoid it in every possible way.

bark
his bark is worse than his bite: someone who appears to be fierce, but who is actually quite gentle.
to bark up the wrong tree: to have a mistaken idea about something.

barrel
to have someone over a barrel: to have someone in a position in which they can do only what you want.

bat
blind as a bat: quite blind.
like a bat out of hell: very fast.
off your own bat: to do something without seeking advice.

be-all
the be-all and end-all: the most important aim or end.

beans
full of beans: lively, vigorous.
to spill the beans: to reveal a secret.

bear
a bear garden: a noisy or unruly place or scene.

bearings
to lose your bearings: to lose your way or direction.

beat
beat about the bush: to delay before saying what you really mean.

beaver
an eager beaver: someone bright, cheerful and enthusiastic.

beck
at someone's beck and call: to be at someone's command.

---

animal idioms
Many idioms use mammals or birds in a colourful way. Here are a few:

bats in the belfry: slightly mad.
the bee's knees: someone who thinks they are superior.
raining cats and dogs: raining hard.
in the dog-house: in disgrace.
dog-in-the-manger: someone with a grudging and unwilling attitude.
a dog's dinner: a mess.
donkey's years: a long time.
to get someone's goat: to annoy someone.
to be up with the lark: to get up early.

---

bed
to get out of bed on the wrong side: to begin a day badly.

bee
to have a bee in your bonnet: to persist in pursuing a single idea.

beeline
to make a beeline: to make directly for someone or something.

beggars
beggars can't be choosers: people in need can only accept what is offered.

bell
as clear as a bell: easily heard.
as sound as a bell: in good condition or working order.
to ring a bell: to recall a distant memory.

belt
below the belt: unfair, not following the rules.
to tighten your belt: to spend less in order to save money.

benefit
benefit of the doubt: to treat someone as innocent, despite your doubts.

IDIOMS

best
the best of both worlds: taking advantage of two different situations.

better
to get the better of someone: to overcome or win.
to have seen better days: to be in a worse condition than before.

bird
the bird has flown: someone has escaped.

bite
to bite off more than you can chew: to take on more than you can really cope with.
to bite someone's head off: to shout angrily at someone.

bitter
a bitter pill to swallow: an unpleasant fact that has to be accepted.

blessing
a blessing in disguise: good fortune coming from an apparent evil.

block
a chip off the old block: a child who takes after one of his or her parents.

blood
to act in cold blood: to do something callously.
blood is thicker than water: family ties are strong and should be preferred to outside loyalties.
to make someone's blood boil: to make someone very angry.
to make someone's blood run cold: to horrify someone.

blue
blue-eyed boy: a favourite.
a bolt from the blue: something unexpected.
once in a blue moon: very rarely.

board
to sweep the board: to carry off all the prizes.

boat
in the same boat: in the same situation.
don't rock the boat: don't spoil things which are pleasant or comfortable.

boats
to burn your boats: to allow yourself no means of retreat.

bolt
to make a bolt for it: to run away or escape.

bone
dry as a bone: very dry.
to have a bone to pick with someone: to have something to complain or quarrel about.

bones
to make no bones about: to say openly and without hesitation.

book
by the book: according to the rules.
to read someone like a book: to understand someone's character.

books
to be in someone's good books: to be in favour with someone.

boots
too big for your boots: to think too highly of yourself.

bow
to have two strings to your bow: not to depend on one person or thing.

brains
to pick someone's brains: to find out what someone thinks about something.
to rack your brains: to think hard about something.

IDIOMS

brass
to get down to brass tacks: to deal with the main points.

bread
to know which side your bread is buttered on: to know where your best interests lie.

breast
to make a clean breast of it: to confess everything.

breath
to take your breath away: to astound.
with bated breath: very excited and anxious.
under your breath: in a whisper.

bricks
like a ton of bricks: very harshly and heavily.

broad
as broad as it's long: whichever way it's considered, it makes no difference.

broom
a new broom: someone in a new situation who starts off with great energy and enthusiasm.

brow
by the sweat of your brow: by hard work.

brush
tarred with the same brush: having the same faults and qualities.

buck
to pass the buck: to pass responsibility onto someone else.

bud
to nip in the bud: to put a stop to something before it has really begun.

bull
like a bull in a china shop: behaving in a rough, coarse, clumsy way.

bundle
to be a bundle of nerves: to be in a very nervous, agitated state.

burn
to burn the candle at both ends: to work and play hard.
to burn the midnight oil: to study or work until late into the night.

bushel
to hide your light under a bushel: to be modest and unassuming.

busman
a busman's holiday: leisure time spent doing the same thing as you do at work.

IDIOMS

butter
butter wouldn't melt in his mouth: applied to someone who looks innocent but probably isn't.

cake
a piece of cake: something easy to do.
to have your cake and eat it: to have it both ways.

cakes
to sell like hot cakes: to sell very quickly.

calf
to kill the fatted calf: to give a special welcome to someone.

cards
to play your cards close to your chest: to be secretive.
to put your cards on the table: to be honest and reveal all.

cart
to put the cart before the horse: to do things in the wrong order.

castles
to build castles in the air: to think up imaginary ideas or schemes.

cat
not room to swing a cat: describes a cramped area.
to let the cat out of the bag: to reveal secret or important news.
to put the cat amongst the pigeons: to cause trouble and confusion.

chalk
as different as chalk from cheese: very different indeed.
not by a long chalk: far from it; not by any means.

cheek
to speak tongue in cheek: to speak mockingly or insincerely.

cheese
hard cheese!: bad luck!

cherry
to have two bites at the cherry: to have two attempts at the same thing.

chest
to get something off your chest: to talk about your problems.

chicken
chicken-feed: something of little value.

choice
Hobson's choice: no choice at all.

cloak
cloak and dagger: secret, undercover.

close
a close shave: a narrow escape.

coast
the coast is clear: there's no danger now.

IDIOMS

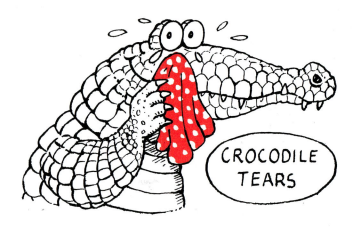

coil
to shuffle off this mortal coil: to die.

colour
off colour: to feel slightly ill.
that's a horse of a different colour: that's quite a different matter.

colours
under false colours: under a false identity.
nail your colours to the mast: to refuse to surrender.

comfort
cold comfort: no comfort at all.

cook
to cook the books: to falsify accounts.

cookie
that's the way the cookie crumbles: you must accept things as they are.

Coventry
send to Coventry: to ignore someone.

creeps
he gives me the creeps: describes a feeling of dislike for, and fear of, someone.

crocodile
crocodile tears: fake tears or sorrow.

cropper
to come a cropper: to fall, usually heavily.

crow
as the crow flies: in a straight line, direct.

crumbs
crumbs from the rich man's table: small trifles given by the rich to the poor.

cud
to chew the cud: to contemplate or think deeply.

cupboard
cupboard love: false affection for material gain.

cut
cut and dried: inflexible and predictable.
to cut a long story short: to leave out the details and get straight to the point.
to cut off your nose to spite your face: to do something in anger which is actually going to cause you more harm.

daggers
at daggers drawn: hostile, quarrelling or fighting.

dance
to lead someone a dance: to cause someone trouble before making a final decision.

dark
to keep dark about something: to keep something a secret.

day
to call it a day: to decide to end something.

IDIOMS

deaf
deaf as a post: very deaf.
to fall on deaf ears: to be unheeded.

deep
to go off the deep end: to get angry and express yourself strongly.

devil
between the devil and the deep sea: stuck between two unpleasant options.

diamond
a rough diamond: a rough person with good qualities.

dice
to dice with death: to perform some dangerous feat.

do
to do someone down: to cheat someone.
to do something up: to restore or repair something.

dog
a dog's dinner: a mess.
dog-tired: very tired.
to lead a dog's life: to have a miserable time.

dogs
go to the dogs: to go to ruin and neglect.
let sleeping dogs lie: to leave well alone.

donkey
donkey's years: a very long time.
he can talk the hind leg off a donkey: someone who talks too much and for too long.

down
down and out: penniless and homeless.

dudgeon
in high dudgeon: angered or annoyed.

dust
to throw dust in someone's eyes: to try to deceive someone.

ear
to get a flea in your ear: to be told off or scolded.

ears
wet behind the ears: lacking in experience.

earth
down-to-earth: practical, plain-spoken.
to the ends of the Earth: anywhere.

easier
easier said than done: it's easier to say how something should be done than actually do it.

eat
to eat like a horse: to eat a lot.

IDIOMS

to keep your end up: to survive under difficulty.

errand

a fool's errand: a purposeless journey.

even

to get even with someone: to have your revenge.

event

to be wise after the event: to offer advice about something after it's happened.

exhibition

to make an exhibition of yourself: to behave foolishly before others.

eye

easy on the eye: attractive to look at.
turn a blind eye to: to ignore an action or behaviour.

eyelid

not to bat an eyelid: to show no surprise or emotion.

eyes

a sight for sore eyes: something very pleasant to look at.
to keep your eyes skinned: to keep a close watch.
up to your eyes: completely.

eating

what's eating you?: what's the matter?

egg

a bad egg: a rascal, someone worthless or unreliable.
to have egg on one's face: to appear foolish.

eggs

to put all your eggs in one basket: to risk everything on one venture.

elbow

elbow grease: hard work.
to give someone the elbow: to get rid of someone.

end

to come to a sticky end: to finish unpleasantly.

face

put a good face on it: to appear to be happy while unhappy.
to face up to something: to accept a situation bravely.
to keep a straight face: to keep serious in an amusing situation.
to face the music: to confront the consequences of an action.

IDIOMS

fair
fair and square: honest and correct.

fall
to fall for: 1. to be deceived, 2. to fall in love with.

false
to sail under false colours: to pretend to be something you aren't in order to gain benefit.

fancy
to take someone's fancy: to take a liking to something or someone.

far
to go too far: to do something unacceptable.

fast
fast and furious: suddenly and quickly.

fat
the fat is in the fire: what has happened can't be changed and the consequences must be accepted.

feather
a feather in your cap: something of which you can be proud.
birds of a feather: people with common interests and tastes.
to feather your nest: to become rich slyly and secretly.
to show the white feather: to be a coward.

feet
to have cold feet: to worry whether you are making the right decision.
to land on your feet: to have good luck.
to stand on your own feet: to be independent.
to sweep someone off their feet: to make a great impression on someone.

fence
to sit on the fence: to remain neutral.

few
few and far between: uncommon, rare.

fiddle
fit as a fiddle: very healthy.
play second fiddle to: to occupy an inferior position to someone.

field
to have a field-day: to enjoy yourself a great deal.

fight
fight tooth and nail: to fight ferociously or with determination.

finger
to have a finger in the pie: to be involved in something.
to twist someone around your little finger: to be able to control or influence someone.

fingers
to be all fingers and thumbs: to be clumsy and awkward.
to burn your fingers: to come off badly.

fingertips
at your fingertips: to be very familiar with something.

fire
to play with fire: to take unnecessary risks.

fish
like a fish out of water: to feel awkward in a strange situation or place.
to have other fish to fry: to have something better to do.

flash
a flash in the pan: something which lasts only a short while.

flat
in a flat spin: in a state of mental confusion.

IDIOMS

fly

fly in the ointment: a small problem or difficulty.

food

food for thought: something worthy of consideration.

fool

to make a fool of someone: to make someone appear silly or stupid.

foot

to have a foot in both camps: to have an interest in both sides.
to put your foot down: to assert your authority.
to put your foot in it: to make an embarrassing mistake.

footloose

footloose and fancy free: free to do anything or go anywhere.

footsteps

to follow in someone's footsteps: to do something which has been done before.

form

true to form: acting in a characteristic manner.

fort

to hold the fort: to look after something while the person in charge is away.

foul

to fall foul of: to have a disagreement with.

frog

to have a frog in your throat: to speak huskily.

frying-pan

to jump from the frying-pan into the fire: to escape from one danger only to encounter a worse one.

furrow

to plough a lonely furrow: to work alone.

gab

the gift of the gab: being able to talk easily and confidently.

gaff

to blow the gaff: to betray a secret to someone in authority.

game

to give the game away: to let a secret out.
to play the game: to behave fairly and honourably.

gate-post

between you and me and the gate-post: in strict confidence.

IDIOMS

ghost
the ghost of a chance: a very slim chance.

gingerbread
to take the gilt off the gingerbread: to reduce the value of something.

give
to give as good as you get: to retaliate as strongly as you are attacked.

gloves
to handle with kid gloves: to treat gently.

glutton
a glutton for punishment: someone who seems to like doing difficult or dangerous tasks.

go
to make a go of something: to make a success of something.

going
to find something heavy going: to find difficulty in making progress.

A FROG IN THE THROAT

gold
to have a heart of gold: to be very kind-hearted.

good
good for nothing: someone useless or worthless.
good Samaritan: someone who gives help to another.
to be up to no good: to be doing something mischievous or wrong.

goose
to cook someone's goose: to ruin someone's chances.

gooseberry
to play gooseberry: to be an unwelcome third when two people want to be alone.

gospel
to take as gospel: to accept something completely.

grace
to fall from grace: to lose favour.
with bad grace: unwillingly.

grade
to make the grade: to succeed.

grain
against the grain: against a natural tendency.

granted
to take something for granted: to assume that something will take place without evidence that it will.

grass
don't let the grass grow under your feet: don't lose time in setting to work.

grave
one foot in the grave: to be old and feeble, near death.
to dig your own grave: to make a situation bad for yourself.

IDIOMS

Greek
it's all Greek to me: it's too difficult for me to understand.

grief
to come to grief: to meet with disaster.

grin
to grin and bear it: to put up with misfortune without complaint.

grindstone
to keep your nose to the grindstone: to keep working without rest.

guess
your guess is as good as mine: I know no more about it than you.

gum
to be up a gum tree: to be in a really bad situation.

gun
to jump the gun: to be too hasty.

hair
a hair's breadth: a tiny distance.
to get in someone's hair: to annoy someone.
to let your hair down: to relax and enjoy yourself.

hairs
to split hairs: to get involved in unimportant details.

hand
an old hand: someone with experience.
don't bite the hand that feeds you: don't be ungrateful to someone who has helped you.
hand in glove: to be on intimate terms with someone.
hand over fist: in large amounts.
to get your hand in: to practise.

handle
to fly off the handle: to lose your temper.

hands
to be in good hands: to be well looked after.
to take your life in your hands: to risk death.
to wash your hands of something: to disclaim responsibility.

hang
to get the hang of something: to understand the principle of something.

hard
hard done by: badly treated.

IDIOMS

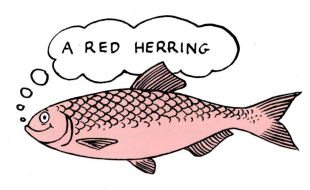

harm
out of harm's way: no longer in a position to cause danger.

hash
to make a hash of something: to ruin a job or project.

hat
at the drop of a hat: right away.
I'll eat my hat: an expression of astonishment.
old hat: out of date.
to keep something under your hat: to keep something secret.
to take your hat off to someone: to show admiration.
to talk through your hat: to talk without real knowledge of something.

hatchet
to bury the hatchet: to end a quarrel.

have
to have it in for someone: to set out to cause harm to someone.
to have it out with someone: to discuss and settle a dispute.

hay
to hit the hay: to go to bed or to sleep.

head
to have a good head on your shoulders: to have good judgment and discretion.
to have a level head: to be sensible and calm.
to keep your head above water: to keep out of debt.
to lose your head: to act stupidly in a crisis.
unable to make head or tail of: unable to understand.

headway
to make headway: to make progress.

heart
my heart bleeds for you: I am very sorry for you.
to break your heart: to feel deep disappointment.
to have your heart in the right place: to be kind and sympathetic.
to take heart: to feel encouraged.
to take something to heart: to feel deeply pained about something.
to wear your heart on your sleeve: to show your feelings openly.

heat
in the heat of the moment: action without thought.

heaven
in seventh heaven: in a state of happiness and perfect bliss.
move heaven and earth: to make every effort.
smell to high heaven: to smell very bad.

heels
to show a clean pair of heels: to escape.

hell
come hell or high water: whatever may happen.
hell for leather: very fast.

herring
a red herring: a false clue or trail.

hiding
he was on a hiding to nothing: he had no chance at all of succeeding.

IDIOMS

hills
as old as the hills: very old.

hog
to go the whole hog: to do something completely and wholeheartedly.

hold
to hold good: to be valid.
to hold in check: to restrain or control.
to hold water: to stand up to close inspection.

holes
to pick holes in something: to find fault with something.

home
to bring something home to someone: to make something fully understood.

hop
to catch someone on the hop: to do something to someone when they are least prepared.

horse
a dark horse: someone who does something unexpected.
to flog a dead horse: to go on discussing something when everyone else has lost interest.
to back the wrong horse: to support the wrong person or party.
to get on your high horse: to be self-righteous and arrogant.

hot
to blow hot and cold: to be enthusiastic and critical by turns.

hour
at the eleventh hour: just in time.

houses
as safe as houses: completely safe.

humble
to eat humble pie: to apologize abjectly.

ice
to break the ice: to ease a first meeting between people.
to cut no ice: to make no impression upon someone.
to put on ice: to postpone.

insult
to add insult to injury: to cause additional trouble to someone.

iron
to rule with a rod of iron: to control someone very strictly.

ivory
an ivory tower: studies or interests which isolate you from other people.

Jack
Jack of all trades: someone who does many jobs but few well.

IDIOMS

jam
in a jam: in a difficult situation.

joke
beyond a joke: no longer funny.

justice
to do justice to: to treat something as it deserves.

keel
on an even keel: calm, steady and untroubled.

ken
beyond our ken: outside our understanding or knowledge.

kettle
a pretty kettle of fish: a muddle or confused state of affairs.
the pot is calling the kettle black: you're criticizing others for faults you have yourself.

kill
dressed to kill: smartly dressed.
to kill two birds with one stone: to gain two objectives with one effort.

killing
to make a killing: to make a large profit.

kingdom
until kingdom come: for a long time.

knock
knock the bottom out of: to prove that a theory or statement is quite false.

knuckle
to knuckle under: to give in, yield.

knuckles
to rap someone over the knuckles: to reprimand.

lamb
like a lamb to the slaughter: quietly, without being aware of any danger.

lap
in the lap of the gods: left to chance.

laugh
to have the last laugh: to have your opinions justified in the end.
to laugh on the other side of your face: to be humiliated.

IDIOMS

law
to be a law unto yourself: to disregard the advice and rules of others.

lead
to lead someone on: to encourage someone by offering false hopes.

leaf
to take a leaf from someone's book: to follow someone's example.
to turn over a new leaf: to reform and start afresh.

leaps
by leaps and bounds: to grow or progress very quickly.

leg
not have a leg to stand on: to have no defence.
to pull someone's leg: to make fun of someone, by telling them something untrue.

light
a leading light: someone important and well-known.
to come to light: to appear or be revealed.
to go out like a light: to drop off to sleep quickly.

lily
to gild the lily: to try to improve something which is already attractive.

linen
to wash your dirty linen in public: to discuss your private business publicly.

lines
to read between the lines: to understand something which is implied.

lion
the lion's share: the largest part.

log
as easy as falling off a log: very easy.

look
to look up to someone: to respect someone highly.

loose
at a loose end: having nothing to do.

love
there is no love lost between them: they dislike each other.

low
to lie low: to hide.

luck
as luck would have it: by fortunate chance.
to push your luck: to take risks.

lurch
to leave in the lurch: to abandon.

luxury
to live in the lap of luxury: to live in comfort and wealth.

mad
mad as a hatter: quite crazy.

make
to make do with something: to use something inferior instead of something better.
to make ends meet: to live within your income.

mark
to be quick off the mark: to be alert and quick to respond.
to be up to the mark: to be of the standard required.

matter
a matter of life and death: something of great importance and urgency.

IDIOMS

meal
to make a meal of something: to make a fuss over something.

mealy
mealy-mouthed: afraid to speak out.

mill
to go through the mill: to endure hard and vigorous training.

million
one in a million: someone or something which is the best of its kind.

mince
don't mince matters: speak plainly and frankly.

mind
to have a good mind to do something: to intend to do something.
to have a mind of your own: to be able to think for yourself.

money
money for old rope: money easily obtained.

monster
the green-eyed monster: jealousy.

mountain
to make a mountain out of a molehill: to exaggerate a problem.

mouth
down in the mouth: distressed or unhappy.

nail
to hit the nail on the head: to understand exactly.

neck
to breathe down someone's neck: to be close behind someone.
neck and neck: equal.

needle
finding a needle in a haystack: attempting to do the impossible.

IDIOMS

nerve
to lose your nerve: to become afraid.

nerves
to get on someone's nerves: to irritate someone.

nest
a nest egg: savings put aside.

nettle
to grasp the nettle: to attack a difficulty with boldness.

nick
in the nick of time: at the last possible moment.

nines
dressed up to the nines: dressed in your best clothes.

nineteen
to talk nineteen to the dozen: to chatter continuously.

nodding
to have a nodding acquaintance: to know someone or something slightly.

nose
to keep your nose clean: to keep out of trouble.
to put someone's nose out of joint: to offend someone.
to pay through the nose: to pay a high price for something.
to turn your nose up at something: to treat with contempt.

numbered
someone's days are numbered: someone or something will not last for long.

nut
a hard nut to crack: a very difficult problem.

nutshell
in a nutshell: very briefly.

oar
to stick your oar in: to interfere.

off
on the off chance: with a slight possibility that something might happen.

over
over my dead body: not if I can prevent it happening!
over and done with: quite finished.

overboard
to go overboard for something: to be enthusiastic about something.

own
to hold your own: to survive against opposition.

oyster
the world is your oyster: to be able to get what you enjoy from life.

p's and q's
to mind your p's and q's: to be polite and well-behaved.

paces
to put someone through their paces: to test someone's ability.

pains
to take pains: to go to a lot of trouble.

paint
to paint the town red: to enjoy life heartily and noisily.

IDIOMS

pale
beyond the pale: outside the limits of decent society.

palm
to have an itching palm: to have a great desire for money.

pants
to bore the pants off someone: to be utterly boring.

pass
to come to a pretty pass: to be in a bad state.
to come to pass: to happen.

path
lead up the garden path: to entice or mislead.

pay
to pay your way: to live free of debt.

peacock
proud as a peacock: vain.

pearls
to cast pearls before swine: to offer something of worth to someone unappreciative.

pebble
you're not the only pebble on the beach: there are plenty of others besides you.

pedestal
to put someone on a pedestal: to have such a great admiration for someone.

peg
a square peg in a round hole: someone in an unsuitable job.
to take someone down a peg: to humiliate someone.

penny
in for a penny, in for a pound: once you've started on something it's best to continue to the end.
to turn up like a bad penny: said of someone unwanted who frequently reappears.

petard
hoist with his own petard: someone caught in a trap which they set to catch others.

PEARLS BEFORE SWINE

Peter
to rob Peter to pay Paul: to pay one person at another's expense.

pillar
from pillar to post: from one refuge to another.

pinch
to feel the pinch: to undergo hardship through lack of money.

plunge
to take the plunge: to take a decision on something risky.

IDIOMS

colour idioms
Many idioms use colours in a descriptive way. Here are some examples:

in the black: in credit.
the future looks black: the future doesn't look promising.
black looks: disapproving glances.
to scream blue murder: to scream loudly.
out of the blue: completely unexpected.
to feel blue: to be depressed.
once in a blue moon: very rarely.
to have green fingers: someone who is good at growing plants.
a red-carpet reception: a lavish welcome.
to paint the town red: to enjoy a night out.
to catch someone red-handed: to catch someone as they are doing something wrong.

pocket
out of pocket: put to expense.

point
not to put too fine a point on it: to speak bluntly.

posted
to keep someone posted: to supply information to someone regularly.

practise
to practise what you preach: you should behave as you tell others to behave.

praise
to damn with faint praise: to praise something so slightly that it amounts to criticism.

presence
presence of mind: having your wits about you.

pressure
to bring pressure to bear: to force someone to do something.

pride
to put your pride in your pocket: to be humble.

pudding
the proof of the pudding is in the eating: only using something decides how useful it is.

pull
to pull through: to succeed with difficulty.

Punch
as pleased as Punch: very pleased.

purposes
at cross purposes: to misunderstand one another's intentions.

put
hard put to it: in great trouble.
to put in a word: to use your influence.
to put off: to postpone.
to put two and two together: to realize something.
to put up with: to suffer.

question
out of the question: not to be considered.

quick
cut to the quick: deeply hurt.

rain
as right as rain: perfectly well.

IDIOMS

rainbow

to chase a rainbow: to think and go after impossible things.

rainy

to keep something for a rainy day: to put something aside in case you may need it later.

rat

to smell a rat: to suspect that something is wrong.

record

to set the record straight: to make sure that any mistake has been rectified.

red

to be in the red: to be in debt.
to see red: to become angry.

rhyme

without rhyme or reason: inexplicably.

ring

to ring the changes: to introduce a new idea.

rise

to take a rise out of someone: to amuse yourself by making someone angry or excited.

rock

steady as a rock: dependable.

Rome

Rome wasn't built in a day: important things cannot be done in a short time.
when in Rome, do as the Romans do: behave like the locals.

roof

to go through the roof: to be very angry.

roost

to come home to roost: refers to a misdeed or mistake which eventually affects the sinner.

A SMELLY RAT

ropes

to know the ropes: to know how to do a particular job.

roses

no bed of roses: a far from comfortable place or situation.

rough

to take the rough with the smooth: to accept set-backs as calmly as you accept good fortune.

roughshod

to ride roughshod: to treat someone harshly and insensitively.

rub

to rub someone up the wrong way: to irritate or upset someone.

rug

to pull the rug from under someone: to cease giving support or help to someone.

IDIOMS

sack
to get the sack: to be dismissed from employment.
to hit the sack: to go to bed or to sleep.

sailing
plain sailing: to continue without difficulty.

salt
salt of the earth: a thoroughly dependable person.

scarce
to make yourself scarce: to vanish or go away.

scenes
behind the scenes: in private.

school
to tell tales out of school: to reveal private or secret information.

scot
scot-free: quite uninjured.

scratch
to start from scratch: to start from the beginning.

secret
an open secret: a secret which everyone knows.

serve
to serve someone right: to be the right punishment for someone.

set
to set about: to commence.

shadow
not a shadow of doubt: no doubt at all.

sheet
to start with a clean sheet: to start anew.

shell
to come out of your shell: to become more bold and confident.

ship
when your ship comes in: when your fortune is made.

ships
ships that pass in the night: people that meet once and never meet again.

shoes
to step into someone's shoes: to take someone's place.

shop
to talk shop: to talk about business affairs.

IDIOMS

shoulder
to give someone the cold shoulder: to be deliberately unfriendly to someone.

shoulders
to be head and shoulders above: far above, or superior to others.

silver
to be born with a silver spoon in your mouth: to be born well-off.

six
six of one and half a dozen of the other: there is no difference or real choice.

sixes
all at sixes and sevens: in a state of disorder or confusion.

skates
to get your skates on: to hurry.

skeleton
skeleton in the cupboard: a secret, usually something of which a person or family is ashamed.

sleep
to sleep like a log: to sleep very soundly.

sleeve
to have something up your sleeve: to have a secret plan which can be used in an emergency.

slip
to give someone the slip: to escape secretly.

smoke
put that in your pipe and smoke it: listen to that and think over it.
there's no smoke without fire: if something is discussed or mentioned, there's usually a good reason for it.

snake
a snake in the grass: a traitor and deceiver.

song
to buy something for a song: to buy something cheaply.
to make a song and dance about something: to make a great fuss.

sorts
out of sorts: not well.

spade
to call a spade a spade: to speak plainly and frankly.

spanner
to throw a spanner in the works: to ruin a plan.

spoil
to spoil for a fight: to be keen to fight.

spoke
to put a spoke in someone's wheel: to hinder someone.

spring
full of the joys of spring: cheerful and happy.

square
back to square one: back to the beginning.

IDIOMS

stand
to stand up for: to support.

steal
to steal a march upon: to gain an advantage over someone.

steam
to let off steam: to give full expression to your feelings.

steamed
to get steamed up: to be angry or upset.

stick
in a cleft stick: in a dilemma.
to stick up for: to support or defend someone.

stomach
to turn your stomach: something that makes you feel sick.

stone
leave no stone unturned: make every effort to do something.
to have a heart of stone: to be hard-hearted.

stools
fall between two stools: to be neither one thing nor another.

storm
a storm in a teacup: big excitement over something very unimportant.

street
right up someone's street: to be exactly right for someone.

strides
to make great strides: to make good progress.

strike
strike while the iron is hot: don't miss a welcome opportunity.

study
in a brown study: completely absorbed in thought.

sweep
to sweep something under the carpet: to hide or keep secret something unpleasant.

swoop
at one fell swoop: in a single movement.

tables
to turn the tables on: to reverse the position of two rivals.

tastes
there's no accounting for tastes: everyone has their own likes and dislikes.

teeth
to escape by the skin of your teeth: to have a very narrow escape.
to get your teeth into something: to tackle something seriously.
to set your teeth on edge: something which irritates you.

tenterhooks
to be on tenterhooks: to feel impatient and anxious.

terms
to come to terms with something: to accept a state of affairs.

tether
at the end of your tether: to reach the end of your resources.

thick
thick as thieves: very friendly.

IDIOMS

thunder
to steal someone's thunder: to spoil the effect of someone's performance by doing beforehand what they intended.

time
for the time being: for the present.
in less than no time: very soon.

toast
warm as toast: comfortably warm.

toffee
toffee-nosed: snobbish or snooty.

tongue
on the tip of your tongue: to be just about to say something.
to hold your tongue: to stay silent.
a slip of the tongue: something said by mistake.

tooth
to have a sweet tooth: to like eating sweet things.

Tom
Every Tom, Dick and Harry: anyone at all.

thorn
to be a thorn in someone's flesh: to cause someone a lot of trouble.

thread
to hang by a thread: to be in a dangerous situation.

threads
pick up the threads: to go back to something after a period of lapse.

thumb
to stick out like a sore thumb: to be obviously out of place.
to be under the thumb of someone: to be totally controlled by someone.

thumbs
thumbs up; thumbs down: acceptance; rejection.

IDIOMS

top
to blow your top: to be very angry.

torch
to carry a torch for someone: to be in love with someone.

towel
to throw in the towel: to admit defeat.

tower
a tower of strength: a reliable and trustworthy person.

trumpet
blow your own trumpet: to sing your own praises.

tune
to the tune of: to the amount of.

twinkling
in the twinkling of an eye: in an instant.

unstuck
to come unstuck: to fail.

untimely
to meet with an untimely end: to die prematurely.

up
to be up to something: to be occupied in some pursuit.

uptake
quick (or slow) on the uptake: quick (or slow) to understand.

vengeance
with a vengeance: extremely.

voice
at the top of your voice: very loudly.

wall
go to the wall: to fail.

wanting
to be found wanting: lacking an important quality.

warts
warts and all: with all the bad points as well as the good ones.

wash
to come out in the wash: to come to a satisfactory end.

water
in hot water: in trouble.
to pour cold water on: to dampen enthusiasm.

waters
pour oil on troubled waters: to bring a quarrel to an end by gentle persuasion.

IDIOMS

way
to get your own way: to have or do what you want.
make way: to stand aside.

wayside
to fall by the wayside: to fail in your endeavour.

weather
under the weather: unwell and not very cheerful.

wedge
the thin end of the wedge: the creation of a dangerous precedent.

weight
to pull your weight: to do a fair share of the work.
to throw your weight about: to be domineering.

whip
to have the whip hand: to have control over something or someone.

whisper
a stage whisper: a whisper that can be heard by everyone.

whistle
to wet your whistle: to have a drink.

white
a white lie: a lie which does no harm, or which is used in politeness.
a white elephant: something which has outlived its usefulness.

whole
the whole shooting match: everything, the whole lot.

wind
to have the wind up: to be afraid.
to sail close to the wind: to come close to causing offence.

wing
to take someone under your wing: to protect.

winks
to have forty winks: to have a nap or short sleep.

wits
at your wits' end: confused and perplexed; not knowing what to do.

wolf
to cry wolf: to give a false warning of danger.
to keep the wolf from the door: to keep yourself alive.

wonder
a nine days' wonder: something which attracts interest but which is soon forgotten.

wonders
wonders will never cease: an expression of surprise at something happening.

wood
not to see the wood for the trees: so concerned with detail that you fail to notice the main idea.

wool
to pull the wool over someone's eyes: to deceive someone.

word
to keep your word: to keep your promise.
to take someone's word for it: to believe what someone says without checking.

words
words fail me: to be too shocked to say anything.

world
on top of the world: very happy and cheerful.
out of this world: excellent.

IDIOMS

worth
to be worth your salt: to be deserving of reward through diligence and hard work.

writing
writing on the wall: an event which foretells future difficulties or problems.

year
since the year dot: for a very long time.

yesterday
to be born yesterday: to be easily deceived.

yarn
to spin a yarn: to tell a story, usually untrue.

ROOTS

ROOTS

The English language is made up of root-words from many different languages. Most of the basic words are from Anglo-Saxon, a Germanic language spoken by the people who came to the British Isles before the Romans. The Romans brought with them the Latin language, and words from Latin began to be used. The Normans, who spoke a type of French, imported words of French origin. Greek words came to English through the Latin language. In this way, English became the complex and rich tongue that it is today. The list that follows gives some examples of root-words that came to English from Anglo-Saxon [A.S.], Latin [L.] and Greek [Gr.].

ac [A.S.], an oak.
acorn.
acer [L.], sharp.
acrid, acrimony, vinegar, eager.
acoustos [Gr.], a hearer, listener.
acoustic.
aedes [L.], a building.
edifice, edify.
aequus [L.], equal.
equal, equality, equator, equinox, adequate.
ager [L.], a field.
agriculture, agrarian, peregrinate.
ago (actum) [L.], I do, I act.
act, agent, agile, agitate, cogent.
agon [Gr.], a contest, mental struggle.
agony, antagonist.
alo [L.], I nourish.
aliment, alimony.
alter [L.], the other of two.
alternative, subaltern, altercation.
altus [L.], high.
altitude, exalt, alto (highest male voice), altar.
ambulo [L.], I walk.
amble, perambulator.
amicus [L.],
amiable, amicable, inimical.
amo [L.], I love.
amity, amorous.
amphis [Gr.], on both sides, both kinds.
amphitheatre, amphibian.
angelos [Gr.], a messenger.
angel, evangelist.
angulus [L.], a corner.
angle, triangle, quadrangle.
anima [L.], life.
animal, animate.
animus [L.], mind.
magnanimity, equanimity, unanimous.
annus [L.], a year.
annual, perennial, biennial, anniversary.
ante [L.], before.
antecede, antediluvian, anteroom.
anthropos [Gr.], a man.
misanthrope, anthropology.
anti [Gr.], opposite, before.
anticlimax, antibody, anti-clockwise.
aperio (apertum) [L.], I open.
aperient, aperture, April (the 'opening' month).
appello [L.], I call.
appeal, appellation, appellant, peal.
aqua [L.], water.
aqueduct, aquatic, aquarium.
arbor [L.], tree.
arboriculture, arboretum.
archo [Gr.], I begin, I rule.
monarch, archaic, archbishop.

ROOTS

arcus [L.], a bow, arch, curve.
arch, arc, arcade.
ardeo [L.], I burn.
ardent, ardour, arson.
aristos [Gr.], best.
aristocrat, aristocracy.
arithmos [Gr.], number.
arithmetic.
ars (artis) [L.], art, skill.
artist, artisan, artifice, inert.
aster or **astron** [Gr.], a star.
astronomy, astrology, asteroid, disaster.
atmos [Gr.], vapour.
atmosphere.
audio [L.], I hear.
audience, audible, auditory.
augeo (auctum) [L.], I increase.
augment, author, auctioneer.
autos [Gr.], self.
autocrat, autograph, automatic.

BEARING A BEAR

bac-an [A.S.], to bake.
baker, batch.
ballo [Gr.], I throw.
ballistics, parable.
ban-a [A.S.], a slayer.
bane, baneful.
bapto [Gr.], I dip.
baptism, baptist.
barba [L.], a beard.
barb, barber, barbel (a type of fish).
baros [Gr.], weight.
barometer, baritone.
bead-an [A.S.], to pray.
bead (originally a necklace or rosary).
beat-an [A.S.], to strike.
beat, bat, battle.
bellum [L.], war.
rebel, rebellious, belligerent, bellicose.
beorg-an [A.S.], to shelter.
burrow, bury, burgh, borough.
ber-an [A.S.], to bear.
bear, bier, bairn, birth, berth, brood, breed.
bet-an [A.S.], to make good.
better, beat (opposite of defeat), best.
biblos [Gr.], a book.
Bible, bibliography.
bidd-an [A.S.], to bid, to pray.
bidding, bead, bode, forbode, forbid.
bind-an [A.S.], to bind.
bind, band, bond, bondage, bundle, woodbine.
bios [Gr.], life.
biography, biology, amphibious.

ROOTS

bis [L.], twice.
biscuit, bisect, bicycle, bivalve, biennial, binary.
bit-an [A.S.], to bite.
bite, bit, beetle, bait, bitter.
blaec [A.S.], pale.
bleak, bleach.
blaw-an [A.S.], to puff.
blow, blast, blare, blot, bloat, bladder.
blostma [A.S.], to blossom.
blossom.
brad [A.S.], broad.
broad, breadth, broadside.
brec-an [A.S.], to break.
break, breakers, brake, breach brittle.
breow-an [A.S.], to brew.
brew, brewer. brewery, broth.
brevis [L.], short.
brevity, abbreviate, brief, breviary, abridge.
bu-an [A.S.], to dwell, to till.
boor, neighbour, bower.
bug-an [A.S.], to bend or bow.
bow, elbow, bough.
byrn-an [A.S.], to burn.
burn, brown, brimstone, brand, burnish.

cado (casum) [L.], I fall.
casual, casualty, accident.
caedo (caesum) [L.], I cut, I kill.
precise, excision, decide, suicide.
calos [Gr.], beautiful.
calligraphy, kaleidoscope.
candeo [L.], I shine, glow.
candle.
candidus [L.], white.
candidate (Roman candidates for office wore white togas), candid.
cano (cantum) [L.], I sing.
cant, canticle, incantation, chant.
capio (captum) [L.], I take.
captive, capture, accept, reception, capacity.
caput [L.], the head.
capital, captain, cape, chapter.
caro (carnis) [L.], flesh.
carnal, carnival, carnivorous, carnation (flesh colour).

ROOTS

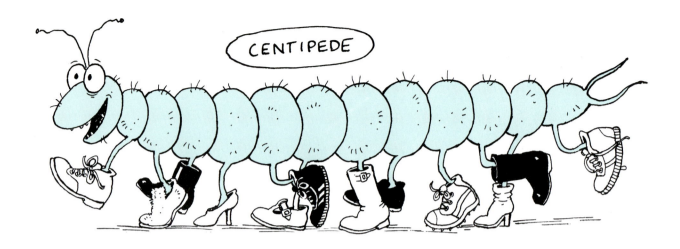

cata [Gr.], down, thoroughly, fully.
catastrophe, catalogue, cataclysm.
catt [A.S.], a cat.
cat, kitten, catkin, caterpillar.
causa [L.], a cause, charge.
causative, accuse, excuse.
caveo (cautum) [L.], I guard against.
caution, precaution.
cavus [L.], hollow.
cave, cavity, excavate, concave.
ceapi-an [A.S.], to buy.
cheap, cheapen, chap, chapman (trader).
cearci-an [A.S.], to crack.
crack, creak, crackle, cricket (insect).
cedo (cessum) [L.], I go, I yield.
proceed, ancestor, secede, cede, concede, intercede, precede, exceed, predecessor.
centrum [L.], (centron [Gr.]), a point, centre.
centre, central, eccentric.
centum [L.], a hundred.
cent, century, centenary, centigrade, centipede, centurion (Roman 'captain of a hundred men').
ceow-an [A.S.], to chew.
chew, cheek, jaw.
cerno (cretrum) [L.], to distinguish.
discern, discretion, discreet.

charis [Gr.], favour.
eucharist.
cheir [Gr.], the hand.
surgeon (formerly chirurgeon), chiropodist.
chole [Gr.], bile.
melancholy, cholera.
chrio [Gr.], I anoint.
Christ, christen.
chroma [Gr.], colour.
chrome, chromatic, chromium, polychromatic.
chronos [Gr.], time.
chronology, chronic, chronicle.
cineticos [Gr.], putting in motion.
kinetic, cinema.
cingo (cinctum) [L.], I encircle.
cincture, succinct, precinct.
cito [L.], I call or summon.
citation, recite, excite, incite.
civis [L.], a citizen.
city, civil, civic, civilize, civilian.
clamo [L.], I shout.
claim, clamour, reclaim, proclamation.
clarus [L.], clear, bright.
clear, clarify, declare, clarion, claret.
claudo (clausum) [L.], I shut.
clause, close, exclude, seclusion.
cleov-an [A.S.], to split.
cleave, cleaver, cleft, clover (split grass).

ROOTS

clifi-an [A.S.], to stick to.
cleave, clip, claw, club.
climax [Gr.], ladder.
climax, climactic.
cline [Gr.], bed.
clinic, clinical.
clino [L.], I bend.
incline, decline, recline.
cnaw-an [A.S.], to know.
know, ken, knowledge.
cnotta [A.S.], a knot.
knot, knit, net.
colo (cultum) [L.], I till, tend.
cultivate, arboriculture, agriculture.
cor (cordis) [L.], the heart.
courage, cordial, discord, record.
corona [L.], a crown.
crown, coronet, coroner, coronation.
corpus [L.], the body.
corps, corpse, corpulent, corporation.
cosmos [Gr.], order.
cosmos, cosmonaut, cosmography, cosmetic.
cratia [Gr.], power.
democracy, autocracy, aristocrat.
credo [L.], I believe, put trust in.
credibility, credence, creditor, creed.
creo [L.], I create.
create, creation, recreation, creature.
cresco [L.], I grow.
increase, decrease, increment, crescent.
criticos [Gr.], to discern, decide.
critic, criterion, hypocrite.
crux (crucis) [L.], a cross.
crucial, crucifix, cruise.
cubo [L.], I lie down, recline.
incubate, recumbent, cubicle.
culpa [L.], a fault.
culprit, culpable, inculpate.
cunn-an [A.S.], to know or to be able.
can, con, cunning, uncouth.
cuon (cun-os) [Gr.], a dog.
cynic (dog-like or churlish), cynicism.
cura [L.], cure, care, concern.
curate, curator, accurate, secure, cure.
curro (cursum) [L.], I run.
course, current, recur, excursion, occur.
cweth-an [A.S.], to say.
quoth, bequeath.
cwic [A.S.], alive.
quicksilver, quicklime.
cyclos [Gr.], a circle.
cycle, cyclone, bicycle.
cynd [A.S.], nature.
kind, kindred, kindly.
cynn [A.S.], tribe.
kin.

A CREATED CREATURE

ROOTS

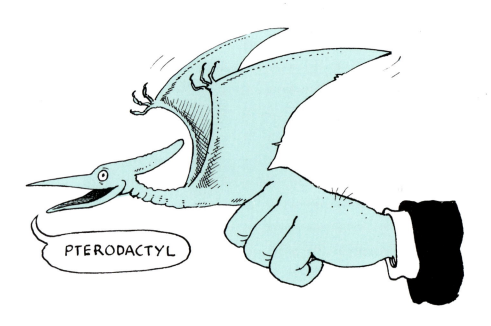

D

dactylos [Gr.], a finger.
dactyl, pterodactyl, date (fruit).
dael-an [A.S.], to divide.
deal, dole, dale, dell.
deca [Gr.], ten.
decagon, decalogue, decade.
decem [L.], ten.
decimal, decimate, December (the tenth month in the Roman calendar).
dem-an [A.S.], to judge.
deem, doom, doomsday, kingdom.
demos [Gr.], the people.
democracy, endemic, epidemic.
dens (dentis) [L.], a tooth.
dentist, dental, indent.
deor [A.S.], dear.
darling, dear, endear, dearth.
derma [Gr.], skin.
dermatology, dermatitis, epidermis.
deus [L.], god.
deity, deify, divine.
dico (dictum) [L.], I say.
verdict, dictionary, dictation, indictment, ditto.
dies [L.], a day.
diary, diurnal, meridian.
dignus [L.], worthy.
dignity, dignify, indignant, deign.
diluvium [L.], flood.
antediluvian.
do (datum) [L.], I give.
date, data, donor, donate, tradition.
doan [A.S.], to act or do.
do, doff, deed.
doceo (doctum) [L.], I teach.
docile, doctor, doctrine.
dogma or **doxa** [Gr.], an opinion.
orthodox, dogma, dogmatic.
domina [L.], mistress of the house.
dame, damsel.
dominus [L.], a lord.
dominate, domineer, dominion.
domus [L.], a house.
domestic, domicile.
dormio [L.], I sleep.
dormitory, dormant, dormouse.
drag-an [A.S.], to draw.
draw, drag, dray, drain, dredge, drawl.
drao [Gr.], I do, act.
drama, dramatic, melodrama.
drif-an [A.S.], to push or drive.
drive, drove, drift, adrift.

ROOTS

Words which have changed their meaning:

acre now a measure of area, once meant simply 'a field'.
clown once meant simply 'a countryman or peasant'.
cunning, which means 'artful or sly', used to mean 'knowing and clever'.
exorbitant originally meant 'out of the way' or 'uncommon', although nowadays it is used to mean 'extravagant and expensive'.
extravagant originally meant 'wandering', while today it means 'to spend money excessively'.
fond which now means 'affectionate', once meant 'foolish'.
gallon now a measure of capacity, once meant 'a basin, bucket or pitcher'.
gentle once meant 'well-born and of good family', while today it means 'of a mild and kindly nature'.
humility once meant 'a low condition' and now means 'meek and humble'.
knave once meant 'a servant', but now it means 'a rogue'.
libel once meant 'a little book' or 'a short writing', but today it means 'a false and damaging statement'.
martyr originally meant 'a witness', but nowadays it means 'someone who suffers greatly, or who dies for a cause'.
nice once meant 'hard to please' or 'very particular'.
paradise once meant 'a royal park', but it has come to mean 'heaven'.
preposterous once meant 'to put last what should be first', but now it means 'absurd, ridiculous'.
silly once meant 'blessed'.
triumph, which now means 'victory', once described a special victory procession.
villain once meant simply 'a peasant', but now it means 'a wicked person or rogue'.
yard now a measure of length, once meant 'a wand or stick'.

drige [A.S.], dry.
dry, drought, drugs (dried plants).
drinc-an [A.S.], to soak or drink.
drink, drench.
drip-an [A.S.], to drip.
drip, drop, droop, dribble, driblet.
duco (ductum) [L.], I lead.
induct, education, duke, produce.
duo [L.], two.
dual, duel, duplex, double, duologue, duplicity (two-fold).
dynamis [Gr.], power, strength.
dynamic, dynamite.

eage [A.S.], eye.
eye, daisy (day's-eye), window (wind-eye).
ego [L.], I.
ego, egotist, egoist, egotism.
eicon [Gr.], an image.
icon.
eidos [Gr.], form.
kaleidoscope, spheroid.
electron [Gr.], amber.
electricity, electric (amber becomes charged with electricity when it is rubbed).
emo (emptum) [L.], I buy.
exemption, redeem.
eo (itum) [L.], I go.
exit, transit, circuit, perish.
epi [Gr.], on.
epidermis, epidemic.
ergon [Gr.], work.
surgeon, energy, metallurgy.
erro [L.], I wander.
error, err, aberration.
eu [Gr.], well, pleasant.
eucharist, euphemism, evangelist, eulogy.

ROOTS

French source words

Many words in the English language have come from French, mainly Old French.

abeie abbey
abit habit
acuser accuse, accusation
alouer allow
armée army
armes arms, to arm
avant-garde vanguard
baie bay
berfrei belfry
blancquet blanket
bouchier butcher
boucle buckle
bouterez buttress
bouton button
capitain captain
carpentier carpenter
carpite carpet
castel, chastel castle
celier cellar
chaiere chair
chambre chamber
chanter chant
cheminée chimney
chérir cherish
chevetaigne chieftain
clerc, clergie cleric, clerk, clergy, clergyman
coissin cushion
colier collar
columne column
cortine curtain
cote coat
crime crime, criminal
degré degree
défendre defend, defence, defender
diamant diamond
donjon dungeon
drapier draper
duc, duchesse duke, duchess
eir heir, heiress
ele aisle
enditier indict, indictment
enemi enemy
enjoier enjoy
esmeraude emerald
espie spy, espionage
esquier esquire, squire
estat estate
estrange strange
estudie study
estuve stew
évident evidence, evident
feste feast
fiers fierce
fleur flour, flower
forteresse fortress
fournir furnish, veneer
franc frank
fraude fraud, fraudulent
frère friar, friary
garde guard, guardian
garite garret
gelée jelly
gendre gender
goune gown
gramaire grammar
grenat garnet
grossier grocer
hacher hash
hanter haunt
harmonie harmony
hostel hostel, hotel
idele idol
incenser incense
juge judge, judgment, judging
juste, justice just, justice, justify
laituë lettuce
larcin larceny
leçon lesson
lieu lieutenant
maistre master, mister
maneir manor
marchant merchant
masson mason, masonry
merci mercy, merciful, merciless
moneie money
mortier mortar
moton mutton
mousseron mushroom
navie navy, naval
nun noun
oignon onion

pais peace, peaceful
paleis palace
pastaierie pastry
perle pearl
persone parson, person, personal
pité pity, pitiful, pitiless
plait plea, plead, pleading
porc pork
porsuivre pursue, pursuance, pursuit
pourchacier purchase
povre poor
pris price
proeve proof, prove
propre proper, properly, property
puye pew
quer choir
retret retreat
retroever retrieve, retriever
rostir roast
roy, roial, roialte royal, royalty
salcise sausage
secrestein sexton, sacristan
sege siege
seint saint, saintly
sergent sergeant
sieute suit, suitable
son sound
soudier soldier
tailleur tailor
tenir tenant, tenacious, tenable
ton tone, tune
torete turret
toster toast
triacle treacle
truele trowel
tur tower
turquiese turquoise
vacabond vagabond
vailant valiant
valée valley
veel veal, vellum
veluotte velvet
vernis varnish
vilein villain
voile veil
voirdit verdict
vyn agre vinegar
yvoire ivory

ROOTS

facies [L.], a face.
facial, face, facet, superficial.
facio (factum) [L.], I make.
factory, faction, fashion, manufacture, feature.
far-an [A.S.], to go or travel.
far, fare, welfare, ferry, ford.
fed-an [A.S], to feed.
feed, food, fodder, foster.
feng-an [A.S.], to catch.
finger, fang, new-fangled (catching new things).
feower [A.S.], four.
four, farthing (fourth-thing), forty.
fero (latum) [L.], I carry, bear.
infer, suffer, reference, relative.
fido [L.], I trust.
confide, diffident, infidel, fidelity.
filium [L.], a thread.
file, defile, profile, fillet.
finis [L.], the end.
finish, finite, infinite, final.
firmus [L.], firm, strong.
firm, infirm, affirm, confirm.

NEW-FANG-LED

ROOTS

A NAGGING GNAT

frons (frontis) [L.], the forehead.
front, frontal, frontier, frontispiece.
fugio [L.], I flee.
fugitive, refugee, subterfuge.
fundo (fusum) [L.], I pour.
fount, foundry, fountain, funnel, diffuse.
fundus [L.], the bottom.
foundation, profound, founder.

flecto (flexum) [L.], I bend.
inflect, inflection, flexible.
fleog-an [A.S.], to flee or fly.
fly, flee, flight, flea, fledged.
fleot-an [A.S.], to float.
float, fleet, ice-floe, afloat, flotsam.
flos (floris) [L.], a flower.
floral, flora, florist.
fluo (fluxum) [L.], I flow.
fluent, fluid, flux, affluent.
fod-a [A.S.], food or feed.
food, feed, fodder, foster, forage, foray.
folium [L.], a leaf.
foliage, foil, portfolio, trefoil, folio.
forma [L.], a form.
form, formal, reform, conformity.
fortis [L.], strong.
fortify, fortitude, fortress, force.
fot [A.S.], foot.
foot, fetter, fetlock, fetch.
frango (fractus) [L.], I break.
fragile, fragment, fraction, infringe.
frater [L.], a brother.
fraternal, fratricide, friar.
freon [A.S.], to love.
friend, Friday (from Friya, goddess of love).

gal-an [A.S.], to sing or yell.
nightingale.
gamos [Gr.], marriage.
monogamy, bigamy.
gang-an [A.S.], to go.
gang, gangway.
gast [A.S.], a ghost or spirit.
ghost, ghastly, aghast.
ge [Gr.], the earth.
geography, geometry, geology.
gennao [Gr.], I produce.
genesis, genealogy, hydrogen, oxygen.
gens (gentis) [L.], a race.
gentile, genteel, congenial.
gero (gestum) [L.], I wear or carry.
gesture, suggestion, indigestion.
glaem [A.S.], a gleam.
gleam, glimmer, glimpse.
gnag-an [A.S.], to bite.
gnaw, gnat, nag.
god [A.S.], good.
God, gospel, gossip.
gradior (gressus) [L.], I go.
progress, congress, degree, ingredient.
gradus [L.], a step.
grade, graduate, gradient.
graf-an [A.S.], to dig or cut.
grave, groove, grove, graft, engrave, carve.

ROOTS

gramma [Gr.], a letter.
telegram, grammar, diagram, gramophone.
grapho [Gr.], I write.
graphic, biography.
gratia [L.], favour.
gratitude, ingratiate, gratis.
gravis [L.], heavy.
grave, gravity, grief, aggrieve.
grip-an [A.S.], to seize or grip.
grip, gripe, grasp, grab, grope.
gyrd-an [A.S.], to surround.
gird, girdle, garden, yard.

habb-an [A.S.], to have.
haft, hap, happy, happen.
habeo (habitum) [L.], I have.
habit, able, exhibit, prohibition.
hael-an [A.S.], to heal.
heal, hale, holy, hallow, health, whole.
haereo (haesum) [L.], I stick.
adhere, cohesion.
haima [Gr.], blood.
haemorrhage, haemophilia.
haireo [Gr.], I choose.
heresy, heretic.
halig [A.S.], holy.
holy, hollyhock, halibut.
heald-an [A.S], to hold.
hold, behold, upholsterer.
hebb-an [A.S.], to raise.
heave, heavy, heaven.
hecaton [Gr.], a hundred.
hectometre, hectograph.
helios [Gr.], the sun.
heliograph, heliotrope, helium.
hemi [Gr.], half.
hemisphere.
heteros [Gr.], different.
heterodox.
hieros [Gr.], sacred.
hierarchy, hieroglyphic.
hippos [Gr.], a horse.
hippopotamus ('river-horse'), hippodrome ('horse-race': in Greek or Roman times an open-air theatre for races).
hlaf [A.S.], bread.
loaf, lord (from hlaford *'loaf-keeper') lady (from* hlafdige *'loaf-kneader').*
hodos [Gr.], a way.
method, period, exodus.
homo [L.], a man.
homicide, homage, human, humane.
homos [Gr.], the same.
homoeopathy, homogeneous, homonym.

ROOTS

Words containing the 'gh' combination

Many words in English contain the combination of the two consonants 'gh'. In this list the words have been grouped according to pronunciation. The 'gh' is only sounded where indicated.

The same vowel sound as in *taut*: afterthought, aught, bought, brought, caught, daughter, forethought, fought, fraught, haughty, naught, naughty, nought, ought, overwrought, sought.

The same vowel sound as in *show*: although, dough, furlough, though.

The same vowel sound as in *colour*: borough, burgh, thorough.

The same vowel sound as in *cow*: bough, plough, drought.

The same vowel sound as in *scoff*, while the 'gh' is sounded as an 'f': cough, trough.

The same vowel sound as in *shoe*: through.

The same vowel sound as in *raft*, with the 'gh' sounded as an 'f': draught, laugh, laughter.

The same vowel sound as in *stuff*, with the 'gh' sounded as an 'f': enough, lough, rough, tough.

The same vowel sound as in *kite*: blight, delight, enlighten, eyesight, fight, flight, fortnight, height, high, insight, knight, light, might, nigh, night, plight, right, sight, sleight, slight, sprightly, thigh.

The same vowel sound as in *may*: eight, inveigh, neigh, weigh, weight.

hydro [Gr.], water.
   hydraulic, hydrophobia, hydrogen.
hyper [Gr.], above, over and beyond.
   hyperbole, hypercritical, hyperspace.
hypnos [Gr.], sleep.
   hypnotism, hypnotic.
hypo [Gr.], under.
   hypocrisy, hypothesis, hypotenuse.

ichthus [Gr.], a fish.
   ichthyology, ichthyosaur.
idios [Gr.], your own.
   idiom, idiot, idiosyncrasy.
ignis [L.], fire.
   ignite, igneous.
impero [L.], I command.
   imperial, imperative, empire, emperor.
initium [L.], a beginning.
   initiate, initial, initiative.
insula [L.], an island.
   isle, insular, peninsula, insulate.
isos [Gr.], equal.
   isobar, isosceles, isotope.

jacio (jectum) [L.], I throw.
   adjective, project, injection, reject, projectile.
judex (judicis) [L.], a judge.
   judgment, judicial, judge.
jungo (junctum) [L.], I join.
   junction, juncture, conjoin, adjunct.
jus (juris) [L.], right.
   justice, jury, injury.

ROOTS

labor (lapsus) [L.], I slide or slip.
lapse, relapse, collapse.
laet [A.S.], slow.
late, latter, last.
lapis (lapidis) [L.], a stone.
lapidary, dilapidated.
laus (laudis) [L.], praise.
laud, laudable.
leac [A.S.], leek.
leek, garlic.
lego [Gr.], I gather, I choose.
eclectic.
lego (lectum) [L.], I gather, read or choose.
collect, elector, select, lecture, legend.
lego (legatum) [L.], I send, appoint.
legate, delegate, legacy.
levis [L.], light.
levity, alleviate, relief, lever, leaven.
lex (legis) [L.], a law.
legal, legislate, legitimate.
lexis [Gr.], word.
lexicon, dyslexia.
liber [L.], a book.
library, libretto.
liber [L.], free.
liberal, liberate, liberty.
licg-an [A.S.], to lie.
lie, lay, layer, lair, outlay.
ligo [L.], I bind.
ligament, religion, oblige, liable.
linquo (lictum) [L.], I leave.
relinquish, relict, relics.
lithos [Gr.], a stone.
lithography, aerolite, monolith.
littera [L.], a letter.
literal, literary, literature.
locus [L.], a place.
local, allocate, dislocate, locomotive.

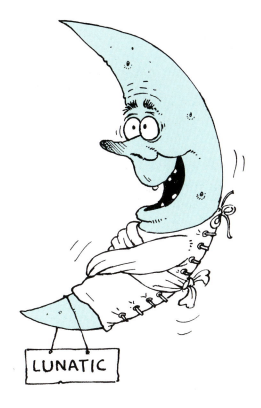

LUNATIC

loda [A.S.], a guide.
lead, leader, lodestone.
logos [Gr.], a word, speech.
logic, dialogue, geology, analogous, physiology.
longus [L.], long.
longevity, longitude, oblong, prolong, lunge.
loquor (locutus) [L.], I speak.
loquacious, elocution, soliloquy.
ludo (lusum) [L.], I play.
elude, illusion, interlude, ludicrous.
lumen [L.], light.
illuminate, luminous, luminary.
luna [L.], the Moon.
lunar, lunatic.
luo [Gr.], I loosen.
paralysis, analysis.
luo (lutum) [L.], I wash.
ablution, dilute.
lux (lucis) [L.], light.
lucid, elucidate.

ROOTS

macros [Gr.], long, large.
macrocosm, macro-lens.
mag-an [A.S.], to be able.
may, main, might, mighty.
magnus [L.], great.
magnitude, magnify, magnificent, magnanimous.
malus [L.], bad.
malady, malice, malaria, malevolent.
maneo (mansum) [L.], remain.
manse, mansion, permanent.
mang [A.S.], a mixture.
among, mongrel, mingle.
manus [L.], the hand.
manuscript, manual, manufacture.
mare [L.], the sea.
marine, mariner, maritime, submarine.
mater [L.], mother.
maternal, matron, matriculate.
maturus [L.], ripe.
mature, immature, premature.
maw-an [A.S.], to cut or mow.
mow, aftermath, mead, meadow.
medius [L.], the middle.
medium, mediate, immediate, Mediterranean.

megas [Gr.], great.
megaphone, megalomania.
melos [Gr.], song.
melodrama, melody.
memini [L.], I remember.
memory, memoir.
memor [L.], remembering.
commemorate, immemorial.
mens (mentis) [L.], the mind.
mental, demented.
mergo (mersum) [L.], I dip, plunge.
emerge, merge, immersion.
merx (mercis) [L.], goods.
merchant, merchandise, commerce, commercial.
meter [Gr.], a mother.
metropolis.
metron [Gr.], a measure.
metre, barometer, diameter, thermometer.
micros [Gr.], small.
microscope, microphone, microfilm, microcosm, microlight.
miles (milites) [L.], soldier.
military, militant, militia.
miror [L.], I admire, wonder at.
admirable, miracle, mirage.
mitto (missum) [L.], I send.
commit, missile, mission, remittance.
modus [L.], a measure.
mood, modify.
mon-a [A.S.], the Moon.
month, moonshine, Moon.
moneo (monitum) [L.], I advise, remind.
monitor, monument, admonish.
monos [Gr.], alone.
monastery, monogram, monarch, monopoly.
mons (montis) [L.], a mountain, mount.
dismount, promontory.
morphe [Gr.], shape.
metamorphosis, amorphous.
mors (mortis) [L.], death.
mortal, immortality, mortify, mortgage, murder.

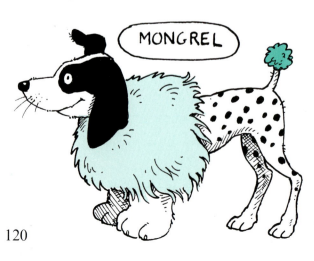

ROOTS

moveo (motum) [L.], I move.
mobile, promote, motor, motion, motive.
multus [L.], many.
multitude, multiple, multiply.
munus (muneris) [L.], a gift.
remuneration, munificent, municipal.
muto [L.], I change.
mutable, transmute, mutation.

novus [L.], new.
novel, renovate, novelty, innovation.
nox (noctis) [L.], night.
nocturnal, equinox.
nudus [L.], naked.
nude, denude, nudity.
numerus [L.], a number.
numeration, innumerable, enumerate, numerous.

naeddre [A.S.], a snake.
adder (originally 'nadder').
nascor (natus) [L.], to be born.
nascent, natal, native, nature.
nasu [A.S.], a nose.
nose, nostril, nosegay.
naus [Gr.], a ship.
nausea.
nauticus [L.], nautical.
nautical.
nautilos [Gr.], a seaman, sailor.
nautilus.
navis [L.], a ship.
navy, naval, navigate, nave (of a church).
necros [Gr.], a dead body.
necropolis, necromancy.
necto (nectum) [L.], I tie.
connect, connection, annex.
nego (negatum) [L.], I deny.
negative, negation, renegade.
neos [Gr.], new.
neologism, neophyte, neolithic.
noceo [L.], I injure.
noxious, innocuous, innocent.
nomen [L.], a name.
nomination, nominal.
nomos [Gr.], a law.
autonomous, astronomy, economy.

octo [L.], eight.
octave, octagon, October (the eighth month in the Roman calendar).
oicos [Gr.], a house.
economy, economical.
omnis [L.], all.
omnibus, omnipotent, omnivorous.
onoma [Gr.], a name.
anonymous, synonym.
optomai [Gr.], I see.
optical, optician.
opus (operis) [L.], work.
operation, co-operation, opera.
ordo (ordinis) [L.], order.
ordinary, ordinance, ordinal, order.
oro [L.], I pray.
oration, orator, oratory.
orthos [Gr.], right.
orthodox, orthography.

pais (paid-os) [Gr.], a boy or child.
pedagogue, paediatrician.
palaeos [Gr.], old.
palaeolithic.

ROOTS

pan [Gr.], all.
pantheist, pantomime, pandemonium, pan-American.

pando (pansum or passum) [L.], I spread out or extend.
expand, expanse.

pareo [L.], I appear.
appear, appearance, apparent, apparition.

paro (paratum) [L.], I put out or prepare.
repair, apparatus, comparison.

pars (pastum) [L.], I feed.
pastor, repast, pasture.

passus [L.], a step.
pace, compass.

pater [L.], a father.
paternal, patrimony, paternity, patron.

pathos [Gr.], feeling.
pathetic, sympathy.

patior (passus) [L.], I suffer.
patient, impatient, passion, passive.

pax (pacis) [L.], peace.
pacific, pacify, pacifist.

pello (pulsum) [L.], I drive.
repel, expel, impel, expulsion, impulsive.

pendeo (pensum) [L.], I hang.
pendant, depend, suspend, suspense, appendix.

penn-an [A.S.], to enclose.
pen, pin, pound, pond, impound.

pente [Gr.], five.
pentagon, pentecost, pentameter pentathlon, pentatonic.

pes (pedis) [L.], the foot.
pedal, impede, pedestrian, biped, centipede.

peto (petitum) [L.], I seek.
petition, compete, appetite.

petra [Gr.], a rock.
petrify, petrel, petroleum, Peter.

phago [Gr], I consume, destroy.
phagocyte, sarcophagus ('flesh-devouring').

phainomal [Gr.], I appear.
phenomenon, fantasy, phantom, fantastic.

phileo [Gr.], I love.
philosophy, philanthropic, philharmonic, philately.

phobos [Gr.], fear.
hydrophobia, claustrophobia.

phone [Gr.], a sound.
phonic, phonetic, symphony, telephone.

phos (photos) [Gr.], light.
photograph, photometer, photogravure.

physis [Gr.], nature.
physics, physiology, physician.

pic [A.S.], a point.
pike, peak, peck.

pilosus [L.], hairy.
caterpillar.

planus [L.], level.
plan, plane, plain.

plastos [Gr.], modelled.
plastic.

plaudo (plausum) [L.], I applaud.
applaud, plausible, explode.

pleo (pletum) [L.], I fill.
complete, complement, supplement, replete.

plico (plicatum) [L.], I fold.
complicate, pliable, reply, display, simple ('one-fold').

poena [L.], punishment.
penal, penitent, penance, repent.

poieo [Gr.], I make.
poet, poetic.

polis [Gr.], a city.
metropolis.

polys [Gr.], many.
polygamy, polyanthus, polytechnic, polychromatic.

pono (positum) [L.], I place.
position, imposition, post, depose.

pons (pontis) [L.], bridge.
pontoon, punt.

Prefixes

ad- towards, to: as in *adjoin, adhere, adjust, advance.*
al- all: as in *almighty, alone, almost, already, always, although.*
amb- on both sides, around: as in *ambiguous, amputate.*
ante- before in time or position: as in *antedate, anteroom, anterior.*
anti- opposed to, against: as in *antidote, antipodes, antipathy, antibiotic.*
bi- or **bin-** two, twice or both: as in *bicentenary, bilateral, bilingual, bicycle.*
by- or **bye-** secondary, near or incidental: as in *bypass, bye-law, bystander, byword.*
co- together, jointly: as in *co-operate, coeducation, coalesce.*
col-, com-, con- and **cor-** together, with: as in *collateral, collect; compute, compound; connect, conduct; correlate, correspond, corrupt.*
counter- against: as in *counterfeit, counteract.*
de- to do the opposite of: as in *devalue, decompose, debase.*
di- double, twice, two: as in *dilemma, divide.*
dis- the opposite of: as in *disagree, disappear, disapprove.*
em- and **en-** into, inside, in: as in *empower, embark; enchant, endow.*
ex- out of, outside, from: as in *export, exclude, excite.*
extra- beyond: as in *extravagant, extraordinary.*
for- reject or forbid: as in *forbid, forswear.*
fore- earlier, before: as in *forefather, forecourt, foreman, foretell.*
forth- forward: as in *forthcoming, forthwith, forthright.*
homo- same, like: as in *homogenize, homophone, homonym.*
im- and **in-** not: as in *impossible, improper; inactive, inattentive.*
inter- between, among: as in *intercept, interfere.*
intra- inside or between: as in *intravenous, intramural.*
intro- into or inward: as in *introduce, introvert.*
mal- and **male-** evil, ill: as in *malcontent, malevolent, malfunction.*
manu- hand: as in *manuscript, manual, manufacture.*
milli- one thousandth part of: as in *millilitre, millimetre.*
mis- 1. wrong or bad: as in *mischief, mischance, misconduct;* 2. lack of, not: as in *mistrust, mistake, misdeed.*
neo- new or recent: as in *neolithic, neologism.*
non- not, the lack of: as in *nondescript, nonsense, nonstop, non-fiction.*
omni- all: as in *omnipotent, omnivorous.*
palaeo- old or ancient: as in *palaeontology, palaeolithic.*
per- through, or throughout: as in *pervade, permanent, perceive.*
post- after, later than: as in *postpone, postdate, posthumous.*
pre- before: as in *precede, predict, prefix.*
pseudo- false or pretended: as in *pseudonym, pseudo-science.*
quadr- four: as in *quadrangle, quadruple, quadruped.*
re- again, repeated: as in *rearrange, react, recall, recite.*
retro- backwards: as in *retrograde, retrospective.*
semi- half: as in *semicolon, semicircle, semi-detached.*
sub- under or beneath: as in *subject, subscribe, sub-standard.*
super- above or over: as in *superior, supersonic, superimpose.*
trans- beyond, over, across, on the other side: as in *transmit, transfer, trans-atlantic.*
un- not: as in *unable, unbend, uncharted, unconscious.*
vice- instead of: as in *vice-president, viceroy.*
with- against, back: as in *withstand, withdraw, withhold.*

ROOTS

porto [L.], I carry.
portable, export, deportment, import, report.

possum [L.], I am able.
possible, impossible.

potens [L.], able.
potential, potent, impotent.

pous (pod-os) [Gr.], a foot.
antipodes, tripod.

prehendo (prehensum) [L.], I take, grasp.
comprehend, comprise, apprentice.

primus [L.], first.
primary, primitive, primrose, prime.

pro [Gr.], before.
proboscis, prologue.

probo [L.], I try, test, prove.
prove, probe, probable, improve.

proprius [L.], your own.
proper, property, appropriate.

protos [Gr.], first.
prototype, protoplasm, protocol, proton.

pseudos [Gr.], a falsehood.
pseudonym.

pungo (punctum) [L.], I prick.
pungent, expunge, punctual.

puto (putatum) [L.], I cut, think.
compute, count, amputate, reputation.

pyr [Gr.], fire.
pyrotechnic, pyre.

quadra [L.], a square.
quadrant, quadratic, quadrille, quarry.

quatuor [L.], four.
quart, quarter.

radix [L.], a root.
radical, eradicate, radish.

raed-an [A.S.], to read or guess.
read, riddle.

rapio (raptum) [L.], I seize.
rapture, surreptitious.

reaf [A.S.], clothing or spoils.
rob, robber; reave, bereave, robe.

rec-an [A.S.], to heed.
reckless, reckon.

rego (rectum) [L.], I rule.
regal, regulate, regent, rector, realm.

rex (regis) [L.], a king.
king.

rheo [Gr.], I flow.
rhetoric, catarrh, rheumatism.

rotate rotund round rotary

124

rideo (risum) [L.], I laugh.
ridicule, deride, ridiculous, risible.
ripe [A.S.], ripe.
ripe, reap.
rogo (rogatum) [L.], I ask.
interrogation, derogatory.
rota [L.], a wheel.
rotate, rotund, round, rotary.
rumpo (ruptum) [L.], I break.
rupture, eruption, disruption.

sacer [L.], sacred.
sacred, sacrament, sacrilege.
salio (saltum) [L.], I leap.
sally, assail, salient, salmon.
sanctus [L.], holy.
sanctuary, saint, sanctimonious, sanctify.
scala [L.], a ladder.
scale, escalation.
scando (scansum) [L.], I climb.
ascension, scan, descend.
sceot-an [A.S.], to throw.
shoot, shot, shut, sheet (thrown over a bed), shuttle.
scer-an [A.S.], to cut or separate.
shear, share, shore, scar, scare, shirt, scrape, scarf, score, sharp.
scio [L.], I know.
science, conscience, ominiscent.
scopeo [Gr.], I see.
microscope, telescope, kaleidoscope.
scribo (scriptum) [L.], I write.
script, scribe, scribble, scripture, inscription.
scuf-an [A.S.], to push.
shove, shovel, scuffle, sheaf, scoop.
seco (sectum) [L.], I cut.
bisect, dissect, section, insect.
sedeo (sessum) [L.], I sit.
sediment, subside, residence, insidious, sedentary.
sentio [L.], I feel.
sense, sentiment, sensual, scent, sensitive.
septem [L.], seven.
septennial, September (the seventh month in the Roman calendar).
sequor (secutus) [L.], I follow.
sequence, sequel, consequent, prosecute.
servio [L.], I serve.
service, servant, sergeant.
sett-an [A.S.], to set or make sit.
sit, set, seat, settle, saddle.
siccus [L.], dry.
desiccate.
signum [L.], a sign.
signify, sign, significant, designate.
similia [L.], like.
similar, resemble, simulate.
slag-an [A.S.], to strike.
slay, slaughter, slog, sledge-hammer.

ROOTS

Suffixes

-able able, fit for: as in *reliable, eatable, laughable*.
-al having the character of: as in *external, dental, fatal, critical*.
-alia a collection: as in *paraphernalia, regalia*.
-ant a person or thing which does an action: as in *defendant, pendant;* or is in the stated condition: as in *triumphant, arrogant, brilliant*.
-ate full of: as in *fortunate, activate, germinate, affectionate*.
-ation action from a verb: as in *consideration, examination, information*.
-ative concerning a verb or noun: as in *imaginative, indicative, formative*.
-ator a person or thing who acts in a particular way: as in *narrator, percolator, calculator*.
-dom the condition of: as in *kingdom, martyrdom, freedom, wisdom*.
-ent similar to -ant: as in *resident, correspondent, student; efficient, urgent*.
-er a person or thing that does something: as in *speaker, runner, driver, cricketer; toaster, revolver, drawer*.
-ery the art, action or condition of something: as in *bravery, archery, forgery, cookery*.
-et small or lesser: as in *inlet, turret*.
-fast firm: as in *steadfast*.
-ful full of: as in *faithful, wishful, painful, doubtful*.
-fy to make or become: as in *modify, signify, terrify*.
-graph something written or pictured: as in *photograph, monograph*.
-hood state or time of being: as in *childhood, sisterhood, manhood, falsehood*.
-ible similar to -able: as in *terrible, horrible, possible, flexible*.
-ic connected with: as in *comic, fanatic, static, automatic, fantastic*.
-ics study, skill or knowledge, as in *mechanics, physics, politics*.
-ise and **-ize** make or put in a stated condition: as in *criticize, chastise, surprise, idolize, fertilize*.
-ism ideas or principles of: as in *fascism, racism, criticism*.
-ist a person with the ideas or principles of: as in *socialist, florist, humorist, artist*.
-ity the quality or an example of: as in *actuality, neutrality, morality, possibility*.
-ive having a capacity to do or cause something: as in *active, digestive, furtive, offensive*.
-less without: as in *defenceless, helpless, hopeless, speechless*.
-like in a manner, or in appearance: as in *childlike, godlike, warlike*.
-ling small: as in *nestling, gosling, yearling, stripling*.
-ly in a manner, or in appearance: as in *orderly, slowly, carefully, quickly, angrily*.
-ment the result, means or cause of an action: as in *punishment, compliment, instalment, sentiment*.
-ness condition or quality: as in *tenderness, sadness, illness, fitness, correctness*.
-or similar to -er: as in *suitor, victor, elector, inspector, conductor*.
-our state, condition or activity: as in *labour, arbour, honour, splendour*.
-ous having the nature, or full of: as in *spacious, dangerous, ominous, ravenous, enormous*.
-ship form, state or condition: as in *fellowship, worship, hardship, township*.
-some characterized by, having the nature of: as in *tiresome, troublesome, irksome*.
-tion a noun from verbs, indicating state, condition or action: as in *rotation, collection, suggestion, description*.
-ward direction: as in *downward, upward, homeward, wayward*.
-wise in the manner of: as in *clockwise, lengthwise, otherwise*.
-y consisting of, full of, characterized by: as in *sunny, funny, showy, dirty, sleepy*.

ROOTS

slawi-an [A.S.] to be slow.
sloth, slug, sluggard, slack.
slip-an [A.S.], to slip.
slip, slop, slipper, sleeve.
snic-an [A.S.], to crawl.
sneak, snake, snail.
socius [L.], a companion.
associate, social, society.
solus [L.], alone.
sole, solitude, solo.
solvo (solutum) [L.], I loose.
dissolve, solution, resolve, absolute.
sophia [Gr.], wisdom.
philosophy, sophisticated.
specio (spectum) [L.], I see.
aspect, spectator, specimen, spectre.
spell [A.S.], a story.
spell-bound, Gospel.
spero [L.], I hope.
desperate, despair.
sphaira [Gr.], a ball, a globe.
sphere, atmosphere, spherical.
spinn-an [A.S.], to spin.
spin, spinster, spindle, spider.
spiro [L.], I breathe.
inspire, aspire, conspirator.
staelc-an [A.S.], to go stealthily.
stalk, stealth.
statuo [L.], I set up.
statue, statute, institute.
stearc [A.S.], stiff or stark.
stiff, stark, strong, string, strength, strangle.
stede [A.S.], a place.
stead, instead, homestead, steady.
stello [Gr.], I send.
apostle, epistle.
step-an [A.S.], to raise up.
steep, steeple.
stereo [Gr.], solid.
stereoscope, stereotype.
stici-an [A.S.], to stick.
stick, stitch, stake, stock, stockade.
stig-an [A.S.], to climb.
stair, stile, stirrup.

sto (statum) [L.], I stand.
stature, status, statute, state, station.
stow [A.S.], a place.
stow, bestow, stowage, stowaway.
stratos [Gr.], an army.
strategy, strategic.
strepho [Gr.], I turn.
catastrophe, apostrophe.
stringo (strictum) [L.], I bind.
stringent, constrain.
struo (structum) [L.], I build.
structure, construct, obstruct, construe, instruct.
styr-an [A.S.], to direct.
steer, stern, steerage.
sumo (sumptum) [L.], I take.
assume, consume, assumption, consumption.
sundri-an [A.S.], to part.
sunder, sundry, asunder.
sweri-an [A.S.], to declare.
swear, answer, forswear.

ROOTS

T

taec-an [A.S.], to show, to take, to teach.
take, teach, teacher, token, taught, mistake.
tango (tactum) [L.], I touch.
tangible, tangent, contact, contagious.
tech-an [A.S.], to draw or tow.
tug, tow.
techne [Gr.], an art.
technical, polytechnic.
tego (tectum) [L.], I cover.
detect, tile.
tele [Gr.], distant.
telegraph, telephone, telescope.
tell-an [A.S.], to count or recount.
tell, tale, talk, toll, teller.
temno [Gr.], I cut.
anatomy, lobotomy.
tempus (temporis) [L.], time.
temporal, contemporary, extemporary.
tendo (tensum) [L.], I stretch.
contend, extend, attend, tense.
teneo (tentum) [L.], I hold.
tenant, tenet, detain, retentive.

terminus [L.], an end.
terminus, terminate, term, interminable.
terra [L.], the earth.
terrain, subterranean, terrestrial, terracotta.
terreo [L.], I frighten.
terror, terrify, deter, terrific.
tetra [Gr.], four.
tetragon, tetrahedon, tetrapod.
texo (textum) [L.], I weave.
textile, text, texture, context.
thaec [A.S.], a roof.
thatch, deck.
theaomai [Gr.], I see.
theory.
theatron [Gr.], a theatre.
theatre, theatrical.
theos [Gr.], a god.
theology, enthusiast.
therme [Gr.], heat.
therm, thermal, thermometer, isotherm.
thesis [Gr.], a placing.
thesis, synthesis, hypothesis.
thyrel [A.S.], hole.
nostril.
tid [A.S.] time.
Christmastide, time and tide.
timeo [L.], I fear.
timid, timorous.
torqueo (tortum) [L.], I twist.
torture, torment, contortion, retort.
traho (tractum) [L.], I draw.
traction, subtract, contractor, tract.
tred-an [A.S.], to walk.
tread, trade.
treis [Gr.], three.
triangle, trigonometry, tripod, trinity.
trepo [Gr.], I turn.
trophy, tropic, heliotrope.
tres (tria) [L.], three.
trefoil, triangle, triennial.
tribuo [L.], I give.
tribute, tributary, contribution.

truwa [A.S.], good faith.
true, truth, troth, betroth.
tumulus [L.], a swelling or mount.
tomb, tumult.
typos [Gr.], the impress of a seal.
type, stereotype, typewriter.
twa [A.S.], two.
two, twin, twenty, twelve (two plus ten).

unus [L.], one.
unit, union, unite, uniform, unique.
urba [L.], a city.
urban, suburb, urbane.

valeo [L.], I am strong.
valour, valiant, prevail.
vanus [L.], empty.
vanity, vanish, vain.
veho (vectum) [L.], I convey.
vehicle, conveyance.
venio [L.], I come.
venture, advent, convene, covenant.
verbum [L.], a word.
verb, adverb, verbose, verbal, proverb.
verto [L.], I turn.
convert, revert, divert, versatile.
verus [L.], true.
verify, verity, aver, verdict.
via [L.], a way.
deviate, previous, trivial.
video (visum) [L.], I see.
vision, provide, visa, revise, visit.
vinco (victum) [L.], I conquer.
victor, convict, victorious, convince.
vitium [L.], a fault.
vice, vitiate, vicious.

vivo (victum) [L.], I live.
vivid, revive, viands, survive.
voco (vocatum) [L.], I call.
vocal, vowel, vocation, revoke.
volo [L.], I wish.
volition, voluntary, benevolence.
volvo (volutum) [L.], I roll.
revolve, involve, evolution.
voveo (votum) [L.], I vow.
vow, vote, devote.
vulgus [L.], the common people.
vulgar, divulge, vulgate.

waci-an [A.S.], to be on your guard.
wake, watch, awake.
wagi-an [A.S.] to waggle.
waggle, waggon, wain, wave, waver.
wana [A.S.], a deficiency.
wan, wane, want, wanton.
war [A.S.], a state of defence.
war, wary, aware, warfare, ward.
wef-an [A.S.], to weave.
weave, weaver, web, webster, cobweb.
wit-an [A.S.], to know.
wit, wise, wisdom, wistful, witness.
wraest-an [A.S.], to wrest.
wrest, wrestle, wrist.
wring-an [A.S.], to force, to wring.
wring, wrong, wrench, wrangler.
wyrt [A.S.], a herb or plant.
wort, wart, orchard.

zoon [Gr.], an animal.
zoo, zoology, zodiac.

ROOTS

American-British Word List

This is a short word list of American words and their British equivalents. These two varieties of English have evolved through the years, sometimes in America and sometimes in Britain. For instance, the word *fall* was used to mean 'autumn' in England at the time of Queen Elizabeth I, yet it is now known as an 'Americanism'. Some new words have been brought into the language by American-English speakers, and some have crossed the Atlantic to become commonly used by British-English speakers.

American	*British*
A	
airplane	aeroplane
aisle	gangway or corridor
aluminum	aluminium
antenna	aerial
anyplace	anywhere
apartment	flat
ashcan	dustbin
attorney	lawyer
automobile	car
B	
baby carriage	pram
backyard	garden
baggage	luggage
baggage car	guard's van
ball park	playing field
Band-Aid	sticking plaster or Elastoplast
barbershop	hairdresser's or barber
barkeeper	barman
baseboard	skirting board
bathroom	toilet
bathtub	bath
bawl out	tell off
bill	bank note
billboard	hoarding
billfold	wallet
bird dog	gun dog
biscuit	scone
blooper	blunder
blow	1. to get out; 2. to wreck
bobcat	North American lynx
booth	telephone box
boxcar	roofed railway waggon
braids	plaits
broil	grill
bug	insect
bulletin board	notice-board
bumper car	dodgem
busy line [telephone]	engaged
buzz saw	circular saw
C	
cabana	beach hut
cabin	cottage
calaboose	jail
calling card	visiting card
can opener	tin opener
candy	sweets

ROOTS

candy store	sweet shop
cane	walking-stick
car	carriage [on a train]
carfare	bus or train fare
carnival	fair
carry-out restaurant	take-away restaurant
casket	coffin
catsup	ketchup
check	1. bill for food; 2. cheque
checkers	draughts
checking account	current account
checkroom	cloakroom
chips	potato crisps
city hall	town hall
clerk	shop assistant
clipping [newspaper]	cutting
closet	cupboard
clothespin	clothes-peg
cloverleaf	motorway intersection
comfort station	public convenience
comforter	duvet
commuter ticket	season-ticket
conductor [railroad]	ticket collector [on a train]
confectioner's sugar	icing sugar
conservatory	school of music
cookie	sweet biscuit
cookie sheet	baking tray
corn	maize
corn syrup	golden syrup
cornstarch	cornflour
cot	camp-bed
cotton candy	candy-floss
councilman	councillor
counterclockwise	anti-clockwise
cracker	cheese biscuit
crib	cot
cuffs [trousers]	turn-ups
cute	pretty or clever
cutoff	by-pass

deck of cards	pack of cards
derby hat	bowler
dessert	sweet or pudding
diaper	nappy
dicker	haggle
dinky	small and inconsequential

ROOTS

dipper	ladle
downspout	drain-pipe
drapes	curtains
dresser	dressing-table
druggist	chemist
drugstore	chemist and general store
drummer	commercial traveller
dumb	stupid
dumbwaiter	food lift or food trolley
duplex house	semi-detached

eggplant	aubergine
elevator	lift
endive	chicory
engineer [railroad]	engine driver
enjoin	forbid
eraser	rubber
expressway	motorway

fall	autumn
faucet	tap
fenders	wings [on a car]
Ferris wheel	big wheel
to figure	calculate
fill out [a form]	fill in
fire department	fire brigade
fireplug	hydrant
first floor	ground floor
fish dealer	fishmonger
flashlight	torch
flatware	table cutlery
flier	circular [in the post]

float valve	ballcock
floor lamp	standard lamp
flutist	flautist
freeway	motorway
french fries	chips
fresh	cheeky, impudent
funeral director	undertaker
funnies	comic papers

garbage	rubbish
garbage can	dustbin
garbage truck	dust-cart
garters	sock suspenders
gas pump	petrol pump
gas or gasoline	petrol
gear-shift	gear-lever
gimpy	lame
given name	Christian name
gizmo	gadget
grab bag	lucky dip
grade crossing	level-crossing
grade school	primary school
grain	corn
green beans	french beans
green thumbs	green fingers
gridiron	football field
grinder	mincer
grip	suitcase
grippe	'flu
ground beef	minced beef
ground wire	earth wire

H

half note	minim
hash	shepherd's pie
hayseed	yokel
head nurse	sister

ROOTS

to hire	to employ	**jacklight**	lantern
hobo	tramp	**jalopy**	old banger [car]
hogpen	pigsty	**janitor**	caretaker
home	house	**Jell-O**	jelly [dessert]
homely	ugly	**jelly**	jam
hood	bonnet [of a car]	**jelly roll**	Swiss roll
hoosegow	jail	**jellybean**	jelly baby
horse sense	common sense	**jumper**	sleeveless dress or pinafore
huckster	salesman or fairground trader	**jumping rope**	skipping-rope

icebox	refrigerator
in your behalf	on your behalf
inning	innings
intermission	interval
internal revenue	inland revenue
intersection [road]	junction

jack rabbit	large hare
jackass	male donkey

K

kerosene	paraffin
kitchen sideboard	dresser
knee pants	short trousers
kook	an eccentric person

L

labor union	trade union
ladybug	ladybird
lawn party	garden party
legal holiday	bank holiday
license plate	number-plate

OLD BANGER

ROOTS

life preserver	lifebelt
lightning bug	glow-worm
lima bean	broad bean
liquor store	off-licence
lockup	jail
longshoreman	docker or stevedore
lowboy	dressing-table
lox	smoked salmon
lumber	timber

mackinaw	short woollen coat
mad	angry
maid of honor	chief bridesmaid
mail	post
marketing	shopping
math	maths
mean	nasty
molasses	dark treacle
mopboard	skirting-board
mortician	undertaker
mucilage	gum [adhesive]
muffler	silencer [car]
mulligan stew	Irish stew
mutt	mongrel

newsstand	bookstall

oarlock	rowlock
oatmeal	porridge
one-way ticket	single
orchestra	front stalls

outhouse	outdoor privy or closet
outlet	electric power socket
overpass	flyover

pacifier	baby's dummy
panhandler	beggar
pantry	larder
pants	trousers
parakeet	budgerigar
parchisi	ludo
parka	anorak
parking lot	car-park
patrolman	police constable
pay station	telephone call box
pea jacket	duffel coat
peddler	stallholder
peek	glimpse
penitentiary	prison
penpoint	nib
pit	fruit-stone or pip
pitcher	jug
pocket book	purse or wallet
port warden	harbour master
potato chips	potato crisps
pry	prise
public school	state school
pullover sweater	jumper, pullover or sweater
punk	trashy or worthless
purse	handbag
pushcart	barrow

quarter note	crotchet

ROOTS

R

American	British
racetrack	racecourse
railroad	railway
railroad tie	sleeper
raise [salary]	rise
real estate agent	estate agent
realtor	estate agent
redcap	railway porter
refuse can	litter bin
rent	hire
restroom	toilet
retroactive	retrospective
romaine lettuce	cos lettuce
roomer	lodger
rooster	cock
round trip	return ticket
row house	terraced house
rummage sale	jumble sale

Some British and American words sound and mean the same, but are spelled differently. Here are some examples:

American	British
aluminum	aluminium
anesthetize	anaesthetize
center	centre
color	colour
defense	defence
fiber	fibre
gray	grey
harbor	harbour
honor	honour
meter	metre
offense	offence
plow	plough
practice [verb]	practise
skillful	skilful
traveled	travelled

S

American	British
sales clerk	shop-assistant
saloon	pub
scallion	spring onion
sedan	saloon car
shade	window-blind
sherbet	water-ice or sorbet
shingle	sign
shoestring	shoe-lace
shorts	pants
sick	ill
sidewalk	pavement
sirloin	rump
skillet	frying-pan
sleeper [railroad]	sleeping-car
slingshot	catapult
slowpoke	slowcoach
smart	clever
snap [bargain]	snip
snap fastener	press-stud
snarl	tangle
sneakers	training shoes
soda biscuit	cream cracker
soda cracker	cream cracker
solitaire [card game]	patience
someplace	somewhere
speedway	motorway
squash [vegetable]	marrow
stand in line	queue
stoop	verandah
store	shop
storekeeper	shopkeeper
streetcar	tram
string beans	french beans
strip of bacon	rasher
stroller	push-chair
subway	tube or underground
sucker [candy]	lollipop
sundown	sunset

sunup	sunrise	unlisted [telephone]	ex-directory
suspenders	braces		
switch [railroad]	points		

tab	bill
taffy	toffee
tag	label
tag day	flag-day
tape needle	bodkin
teacart	tea trolley
telephone booth	call-box
throughway	motorway
thumbtack	drawing-pin
tick-tack-toe	noughts and crosses
tie [railroad]	sleeper
toque	woollen hat
traction	tramway
to trade	swap
traffic circle	roundabout
trailer	caravan
transom	fanlight
trash	rubbish
trolley	tram
truck	lorry
truck farm	market garden
trunk	boot of a car
tuxedo	dinner-jacket
twister	tornado

vacation	holiday
valance	pelmet
valise	hand luggage
vest	waistcoat
vine	creeper

warden [prison]	governor
washcloth	flannel
weenie	hot dog
windshield	windscreen
wrench	spanner

Y

yam	sweet potato
yard	back garden

underpass	subway
undershirt	vest

Z

zip code	post-code
zucchini	courgette
zwieback	rusk

ORIGINS

ORIGINS

English has developed into the modern language that we speak and write through a long history of influences since the early Anglo-Saxon (Old English) form. The Normans spoke a type of French which became intermixed with Anglo-Saxon, but even before that the Romans had introduced Latin to England. In the centuries that followed, English adopted words from all over the world, and new ones are always coming into use. In recent years *apartheid* (from Afrikaans), *glasnost* and *perestroika* (from Russian) have come into the English language, and this process goes on continuously. The following list gives the history of some interesting English words.

aardvark This name was given to the animal by the Dutch settlers in South Africa. It means 'earth-pig', although an aardvark is actually a kind of anteater.

academy Originally a Greek word from the name of the Greek legendary hero Academus. A gymnasium (school) in the outskirts of Athens was named after him, and was later used to describe other places of learning.

adder is an Old English word *naedre*, meaning 'snake'. The modern German word is *natter*. The word in English lost its 'n' because, when referring to 'a nadder' (as the word once was), the 'n' was mistakenly moved to make the expression 'an adder'.

admiral is of Arabic origin and comes from the word *amir*, meaning 'prince' or 'leader', first used to describe chieftains on land and sea. The letter 'd' crept in because of the similarity to the word 'admire'.

aftermath is made up of 'after' and 'math', the second word being an old English form of 'mowing'. This is because the word 'aftermath' originally referred to a second crop of grass.

agnostic This is quite a new word, invented in 1869 by T.H. Huxley, the scientist. 'Gnostics' were an early Christian sect claiming mystic knowledge, and the 'a' in front denotes 'without such knowledge'.

alcohol is from the Arabic, and means 'fine black powder'. 'Kohl' is still used as eye make-up by many women. Later the word was applied to fine distilled liquids, and finally was used for a spirit of wine.

ORIGINS

alligator comes from the Latin word *lacertus*. The name came to English through Spanish. The Spanish for alligator is *lagarto*, and the Spanish word for 'the' is *el*. When *el lagarto* was heard by English speakers, it sounded like the one word 'alligator'.

ambush comes from an Old French word meaning 'to hide in the bushes', and is taken from an even earlier Roman word meaning 'to put into a wood'. So it has come to mean 'to take someone by surprise'.

anaconda is a word which comes from Sri Lanka, and means 'lightning stem'. It originally described a whip-snake, but was used by mistake to describe a much larger South American boa.

answer is an Anglo-Saxon word, the second half coming from the same root as 'swear'. It once meant to swear a solemn oath in reply to a charge. The first part 'an' means 'against', so the whole word meant 'to swear against'.

apostrophe comes from the Greek, meaning 'turned away', and was once used to mean 'turning aside to address someone'. It was later applied to the punctuation mark meaning something omitted or 'turned away'.

apricot was once spelled 'apricock', and came into English through French, Portuguese and Arabic from Latin. The last half of the word comes from Latin *praecox* 'early-ripe', a word also related to 'precocious'.

archipelago originally meant 'Aegean Sea'. This sea has many islands, and so the word came to mean a number of islands. The word is Greek, formed from *archi* 'main, principal' and *pelagos* 'sea'.

armadillo is a Spanish word meaning 'armed man' or 'little armoured one', which is apt for an animal whose body is almost entirely encased in a kind of protective armour.

atlas comes from the name of the Titan in Greek mythology who was condemned by the gods to hold up the sky. His name was given to mountains in North Africa and to the Atlantic Ocean. In the 16th century the figure of Atlas often appeared in the front of books of maps. Other similar books came to be called 'atlases'.

attorney comes from the French, and is based on the word 'turn'. It applies to someone to whom people turn for help, especially in legal matters.

ORIGINS

badminton is from a place-name. It was named after the country house of the Duke of Beaufort, Badminton House in the county of Avon, England, where the game was first played in the middle of the 19th century.

bald originally meant 'having a white patch' and not just hairless. A common name for an inn in England is the 'Bald Faced Stag'. This phrase meant that the animal had a white patch on its face.

banjo has two possible origins. In Latin and Greek the word *pandura* was the name for a musical instrument sacred to the Greek god, Pan. In Europe, up to about the 16th century, this became a lute-like instrument with the name 'bandore' which became mispronounced as 'banjo'. Another explanation is that 'banjo' derives from the word *mbanza*, a similar instrument from North Africa.

barber comes from the Latin *barba* 'beard', because in early times a barber's work was largely concerned with trimming and cutting beards.

bayonet comes from the town of Bayonne in France, which is where these weapons were originally made. The 'et' ending means something small, as in cigarette 'a small cigar'.

beg comes from the word 'beggar', and not the other way about. The word 'beggar' comes from the Old French *bégard*, a 13th-century begging monk which, in turn, is taken from Lambert le Begue the founder of the Christian sisterhood called the Beguines.

biscuit came to English from French, but the word originates in the Medieval Latin *bis coctus* 'twice baked'.

141

ORIGINS

blackmail The second part of this word 'mail' comes from Scotland, and means 'payment, tax or tribute'. Blackmail is a 16th-century word for the tribute demanded by rebel chiefs in return for their protection.

Bolshevik is a Russian word which comes from the word *bolshoi*, meaning 'big'. A 'Bolshevik' was a member of the majority socialist party. The others were called 'Mensheviks' (from *menshiy* 'less').

bonfire was, in the 14th century, a 'bone-fire' – an open-air burning of bones. Bone-burning was a common event until the beginning of the 19th century, with bones saved especially for the purpose.

boss is of Dutch origin, but first came into English in the United States. It comes from the word *baas* 'master', which earlier had meant 'uncle'.

boycott is named after a person. He was Captain C.C. Boycott, an Irish landlord, who, in the 1880s, was excluded from the Irish Land League after charging his tenants unreasonable rents.

brandy is a shortened form of 'brandywine'. 'Brand' was a word connected with burning, so brandywine means 'burned wine'. In fact the spirit was not burned, but distilled over a hot fire.

bridegroom The 'groom' in this case is nothing to do with horses. In fact, the original word was 'gome', which meant 'man'. The word 'groom' crept in by mistake.

buccaneer comes from the French *boucanier*, the name for a hunter who dried and stored meat on a wooden frame called a 'boucan'. These people were to be found on the island of San Domingo in the West Indies. Later, the word was applied generally to pirates.

bungalow comes from a Hindi word *bangla* meaning 'belonging to Bengal', where thatched, one-storey houses were found.

bunkum is an American word taken from Buncombe, a county in North Carolina. It was used to mean 'nonsense' after a series of inane speeches by the Congressional representative for Buncombe between 1819 and 1821.

butler comes from the Old French word *bouteillier*, describing a man who put wine into bottles. The Normans brought the word to England as *buteler*.

cabinet comes from the same root as 'cabin', meaning a small room. Such a room was often used for displaying works of art, and the word was later applied to a small case used for the same purpose.

calculate comes from the Latin *calculare* 'to calculate', and from *calculus* 'a pebble'. Small stones were used for counting and calculating. The Latin *calx* meant 'a counter' and 'limestone', and is also the origin of our word 'chalk'.

candle comes from a Latin word introduced into England at the beginning of the seventh century as *candela*, from the word *candere*, meaning 'to shine'.

ORIGINS

card comes from the French *carte*, and in turn from Latin *charta*. This originally meant 'a papyrus leaf', and later 'paper'. It was taken from the Greek *chartes*, also meaning 'a papyrus leaf'. Both in English and French, the word 'card' or *carte* was first used of playing-cards.

carol was originally used to mean a kind of dance, the word coming from the Old French word *carole*. This in turn came from the Latin *corolla* 'a garland'. The dance was accompanied by music, and later the word was applied to the music itself.

cashier comes from the French *caissier*, from *casse* meaning money-chest.

castanet has come into English from Spanish as *castañeta*, which in turn comes from the Latin word *castanea* 'chestnut'. Castanets are so-called because of their shape, which resembles a chestnut.

chameleon is a Latin word taken from Greek *chamaileon*. *Chamai* means 'on (or near) the ground' (a dwarf), and *leon* is 'lion'. So the word means 'dwarf lion', although a chameleon is not, of course, a lion at all.

chap once meant 'a customer or purchaser', and is taken from 'chapman' meaning 'a dealer'. In its other sense 'chap' is related to 'chip' and 'chop', the sort of blow which causes a crack.

church comes from Greek, and in English once had a sound like 'k' instead of 'ch'. In Scotland the word 'kirk' is still used. Its origin is in the Greek word *kyrios* 'lord'; so it means 'house of the Lord'.

cliché is a French word, first used in the 19th century for the metal printing block called a 'stereotype plate'. The word *clicher* described the sound made as the mould was dropped into the molten metal. It then came to be used to describe any commonplace phrase, word or idea.

clove If you look closely at a clove it looks very like a nail. The English name comes from the French *clou de girofle* 'nail of the clove-tree'.

clumsy is of Scandinavian origin, where it has several meanings. *Klumsen* means 'to strike dumb' or 'hamper' and also 'dazed, numb'. Its meaning has changed in English.

CHAMELION

ORIGINS

coach comes from a place-name in Hungary called Kocs (pronounced 'koch'). It was here that the *Kocsi szekér* (Kocs cart) was invented in the 15th century. The word has passed into most European languages, pronounced much as in English.

colonel is connected with the word 'column', being the officer who led such a column. Some languages spelled the word 'coronel', which explains why in English it has an unusual pronunciation.

companion is from French *compagnon*. This is taken from the Latin *com* 'with' and *panis* 'bread', producing a word which means 'one who eats bread with another'.

comrade really means 'chamber-fellow', since it comes from the Latin root *camera*, meaning 'chamber' or 'room'. In French it is *camarade*, and in Spanish *camarada*, both meaning 'room-mate'.

confetti comes from Italian and means 'small sweets'. Traditionally sweets were thrown after weddings, and later small discs of paper were used.

constable is from the Latin *comes stabuli*, which means 'officer in charge of the stable'. Governors of royal castles in England and France were given the title 'constable', which was first used to mean 'an officer of the peace' in the 14th century.

copper was, in ancient times, found mostly on the island of Cyprus. The metal took its name *copreum* from the island, whose Latin name was *Cyprium* or *Cuprium*.

cosy is a word of Scottish origin which is possibly connected with the Norwegian word *koselig* 'snug, cosy'. The word in English was once spelled 'colsie'.

cot is a word adopted from India, where it takes the form in Hindi of *khat*, meaning a 'bedstead, couch or hammock'. Such a bed was first used by British soldiers in India, and the word was brought back home by them in about the 17th century.

crane is a bird from which a machine takes its name. Many other animals have given their names to mechanical objects, for example, monkey-wrench, donkey-engine, kite and pig-iron.

crimson takes its name from an insect, the *kermes*, which was once used for making a red dye. The kermes was also known in Spanish and Italian as *cremesin* and *cremesino*, and it was from these that the English word came.

ORIGINS

crook is used to describe 'swindlers' or 'criminals' because they are 'not straight'. It is also possible that our word 'crooked' comes from the Old Norse *krokottr* 'crooked, winding, cunning or wily'.

crusade comes from the French *crois* 'cross', and also from the Spanish *cruzar* 'to take up the cross'.

crypt comes from the Greek, meaning 'a vault', but the root of the same word also means 'hidden'. So in English we have 'cryptic' meaning 'hidden, secret', and 'cryptogram' which is a secret message in code.

currant takes its name from Corinth, in Greece, which was the place from which currants were first sent abroad. The name came into English from France, where the fruit was originally called *raisin de Coraunte*, or 'Corinth grape'.

dahlia is a flower which was named in 1791 in honour of the Swedish botanist Anders Dahl.

damson is taken from the word *damascene*, since this fruit was originally called the damascene plum or 'plum of Damascus'. The fruit was first cultivated in Syria, and so takes its name from its capital.

dean has come to English through Latin from Greek. The word was originally *dekanos*, the name given to a monk or other dignitary in charge of ten others. In Greek *deka* means 'ten'.

decoy comes from the Dutch *de kooieend* 'the duck decoy'. The word *kooi* in Dutch means 'cage'.

deer originally meant any kind of wild animal. Dutch and German still use the words *dier* and *tier* to mean 'animal'.

denarius is the shortened form of *denarius nummus*, a Roman coin containing ten *asses*. The letter 'd' was formerly used in Britain to denote a penny.

denim takes its name from the place where it was made in the 17th century: Nîmes in France. In French, it was known as *serge de Nîmes*.

ORIGINS

derrick has a rather gruesome origin, since it takes its name from the gallows on which criminals were hanged. In about 1600 the surname of the hangman at Tyburn, near London, was Derrick and he gave his name to the gallows there.

diesel takes its name from the inventor of the diesel engine. Rudolf Diesel was a German engineer who patented his engine in 1893, although he never made his fortune from it. He died at the age of 55 after falling overboard from the Antwerp to Harwich steamer.

dinner comes from the French *dîner*, and its earlier form *disner*. This came from the Latin *disjejunare* 'to break fast'. In fact, the French word *déjeuner* 'to breakfast' also comes from the same Latin word.

dinosaur is a word invented in 1841 to describe certain prehistoric animals. It is made up of two Greek words, *deinos* meaning 'terrible' and *sauros* 'lizard', which produces the description 'terrible lizard'.

dismal originally meant 'evil days', referring to so-called 'unlucky' days in the medieval calendar. The word comes from the Latin *dies mali* 'evil days', which became *dis mal* in Norman French, and one word in English.

dollar is a form of the German word *taler* or *thaler*. This is a shortening of 'Joachimsthaler', the name of a silver coin made in about 1518 from metal found in Joachimsthal (Joachim's valley), in Bohemia, in the west of Czechoslovakia. The Spanish eight reales coin was commonly called a dollar, and was used in the 'New World'.

domino The name of the game dominoes probably comes from the Italian exclamation *domino!* meaning 'master' or 'winner'.

dreary comes from the Old English word *dreor*, meaning 'gore, flowing with blood'. Its meaning has slowly changed since the early days.

dromedary literally means 'a fast runner', from the Greek word *dromad*.

ORIGINS

dunce comes from the name of John Duns Scotus, who was far from being a dunce. The word was applied contemptuously to the followers of Scotus in the 14th century by those who opposed his ideas and ridiculed his teachings.

earwig is so called because in early times it was thought (quite wrongly) that the insects could penetrate the ear. The same ideas occur in French (*perce-oreille* 'pierce-ear'), German and Dutch, (*Ohrwurm* and *oorworm* 'ear-worm').

elastic was first used to describe expansion in substances such as gases. It comes from the Greek *elastikos*, meaning 'driving' or 'propelling'. Later, it came to mean 'to resume normal size after expansion'.

EARWIG

electricity comes from the Greek name for amber, *elektron*. This is because amber can be given an electric charge and made to attract small pieces of materials such as paper and cotton after being rubbed.

embargo is a Spanish word and comes from the verb *embargar*, meaning 'to arrest or impede'. An embargo was an order forbidding any ships to leave or enter a harbour, usually when a war was declared.

engine today means a mechanical contrivance, but it once meant 'wit' or 'genius'. It is related to the word 'ingenious', and so also meant 'cleverness'. The idea of an engine being a machine came into the English language in about the 14th century.

evangelist strictly means 'one who brings good tidings'. An angel brought messages from God, but especially good news was carried by an *evangel*. In later times evangelism has come to mean the teaching or preaching of the gospel.

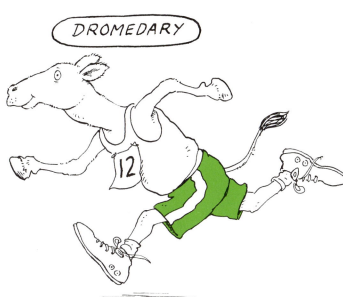

DROMEDARY

ORIGINS

exhilarate comes from the same root as 'hilarious'. This word comes from the Latin *ex* 'out of' and *hilarare* 'to cheer', giving an original meaning 'bringing out happiness'.

explode is a word which has changed its meaning. It came from the Latin *explodere* and originally meant 'to drive out by clapping', or, in the theatre 'to hiss off the stage'.

fad dates from the 19th century, and is a shortening of the earlier expression 'fidfad'. This in turn was a shortening of 'fiddle-faddle', a 16th-century term meaning 'trifling talk or action'.

fan is simply an abbreviation of 'fanatic', someone who has a frenzied manner, and particularly who is madly devoted to an idea. The present meaning of the word 'fan' entered English in the United States in the 19th century.

ferret comes from a Latin word *fur* meaning 'thief', probably because the animal invades the burrows of other creatures. The same root-word is found in the word 'furtive'.

fiasco is the Italian word for 'bottle' or 'flask'. When something goes wrong, an Italian might say 'it has made a bottle', but no-one quite knows why this expression is used.

flabbergast is a made-up word which was first used in the 18th century. It is made up of the word 'flabby' or 'flap', joined to the word 'aghast'.

flour and **flower** both come from the French word *fleur*. In the first word, the French expression was *fleur de farine* or 'flower of wheat'. The spelling 'flower' for both meanings was quite common in English until the early 19th century.

focus is the Latin word for 'fireplace', the central point in a room. It was also used to describe a 'burning-point', such as when a lens was used for focusing the rays of the sun to burn something.

foreign is from the French *forain*, which comes from the Latin *foranus* 'a foreigner'. This in turn is taken from the Latin word *foris* 'outside'.

fortnight is a shortening of 'fourteen nights', as in medieval times periods were reckoned by nights rather than days. There was also an old word *sennight*, meaning 'seven nights', or 'a week'.

franchise originally meant 'freedom', and comes from the Old French *franche* 'free'. It came to have its present meaning (the right to vote) during the 18th century. Before that it meant 'privilege or immunity under the law'.

ORIGINS

G

gaberdine (also spelled *gabardine*) is a type of cloth, but also gave its name to a loosely fitting upper garment.

galvanize takes its name from the Italian scientist, Luigi Galvani, who discovered this process of producing electricity by chemical action in 1792.

gas is a word invented in the 17th century by the Dutch chemist J.B. van Helmont, who took the name from the Greek word *chaos* meaning 'atmosphere'. The Greek 'ch' sound is a guttural one and is represented in Dutch by the letter 'g'.

gingham is taken from the Malay word *ginggang*, which meant 'striped' and was applied to cloth which had stripes. It was used by Dutch traders in the East Indies in the 17th century, and passed onto English and other languages.

glamour once meant 'magic', or 'spell', but by the 19th century had come to mean 'magic beauty', largely due to its use by the Scottish writer, Sir Walter Scott. It is from a 15th-century Scottish word *gramarye* formed from the word 'grammar', meaning 'magic learning'.

gooseberry has nothing to do with the goose, but comes from *groose* which is related to the German word *kraus*, meaning 'curly'. In French it is called *groseille*, and in medieval Latin the plant was known as *uva crispa*, or 'curly grape'.

grapefruit is a word which came into English through the United States. It is so called because the fruit grows in clusters, like giant bunches of grapes. It is also known as the 'pomelo', while an earlier form of the fruit was called the 'shaddock', named from a Captain Shaddock who introduced the fruit to Jamaica from the East Indies.

grenade comes from the French word *grenade*, meaning a 'pomegranate'. The name was applied to this explosive shell because of its resemblance to the fruit. In Old French, the fruit was called *pome grenade*.

grocer originally meant 'a dealer in the gross', or a 'wholesaler'. In London, the Grocers' Company was a group of people who dealt largely in foreign produce, which gave the word its modern sense.

guinea pig has nothing to do with the African country of Guinea, nor does it refer to a pig. The name 'Guinea' was often used vaguely for 'distant country', and the word 'pig' equally as imprecisely for an animal. It is also called the 'cavy'.

ORIGINS

halibut means 'holy fish', the word *butt* being an old Dutch word for all kinds of flat fish. It was so called because it was eaten on holy days. Another name containing a form of *butt* is turbot, meaning 'thorn-fish'.

hamburger is named after the German city of Hamburg. The full expression is 'Hamburger steak', meaning 'steak in the Hamburg style'.

handsome originally meant 'easy or pleasant to handle'. Its meaning was extended to mean 'pleasant', and then 'of pleasing appearance'. It still retains its other meaning of 'ample, sizeable or large'.

harmonica was first used by Benjamin Franklin in 1762 to describe a glass musical instrument. Nowadays it is used as a name for the mouth organ, an instrument dating back to the early 19th century, then called the 'aura'.

hazard is a word which started as the name of a game of dice, but later extended to all kinds of risks. The word comes to English from French *hasard*, through Spanish *azar*. The Spaniards adopted the word from the Arabic word *az-zahr*, meaning a gaming die.

hearse comes from the French word *herse*, describing a triangular iron frame used in church to hold candles. The candle-holder was placed over the coffin in church, and the name was later applied to the frame or canopy containing the coffin, set up in the church or carried through the streets.

helicopter is a modern word made up of two Greek ones: *heliko* meaning 'screw' and *pteron* meaning 'wing'.

hieroglyphic comes from the Greek words *hieros* 'sacred' and *glyphe* 'writing'. The word is found in the writings of th Greek philosopher Plutarch (AD 46–119), meaning 'letters or writing', but it was also used in the 16th century to describe secret or symbolic writing.

hippopotamus is a word taken from the Greek *hippos* 'horse' and *potamos* 'river', although the animal is not related to the horse.

hooligan comes from the name of a rowdy Irish family, called Houlihan, who lived in Southwark in south-east London in the late 19th century. The family was immortalized by a music-hall song popular at the time.

ORIGINS

host comes from the Old French *hoste* (now *hôte*), meaning a host or guest, from the Latin *hospes*. The English words 'hotel' and 'hostel' come from the same source.

humble comes from the Latin, meaning 'lowly' or 'mean'. But the phrase 'to eat humble-pie' has quite a different origin. It comes from 'umbles', the cheaply-bought inner parts of an animal.

husband is a word which once applied to all men who were masters of the household, whether married or not. The word comes from the Old Norse *husbondi* meaning 'someone who has a household'.

idiot once meant simply 'an ignorant person' or 'peasant', and comes from the Greek *idiotes*, meaning a common person or layman.

illustrate originally meant to 'throw light upon', and still retains that meaning in some senses. It had nothing to do with pictures until the 17th century.

indigo is a blue powder dye obtained from the plant *Indigofera*. In the 16th and 17th centuries it was spelled *indico*, having been taken from the Spanish. It comes originally from the Greek *Indikos*, meaning 'of India'.

infantry once applied to a force of soldiers who were too young to serve in the cavalry. It comes from the Italian *infante* meaning a 'boy'. It was only in the 16th century that the word was applied to all foot-soldiers.

insulate comes from the Latin word *insula* meaning 'island', expressing the idea 'to isolate or detach'. Since about 1800 the word has taken on the specific meaning 'to prevent the passage of electricity'.

interfere In the 16th century this word was used about horses and meant 'to strike the fetlock with the hoof of the opposite foot', or 'to knock one leg against the other'. It later came to mean 'to collide or clash', and since the 18th century, 'to intervene'. The word comes from France.

interlude was originally used to describe a short play, dance or piece of music performed in the middle of a longer entertainment. It comes from the Latin *inter* 'between' and *ludus* 'play'.

intoxicate has changed its meaning since the 16th century, when it simply meant 'to poison'. The word comes from the Greek *toxikon* a 'poison for arrows', from the related word *toxon* a 'bow'.

151

ORIGINS

jacket comes from the French *jacquette*, which in turn comes from *jacque*. It is also the personal name Jacques, but in the common use meant a leather jerkin or a leather drinking vessel. In English it was spelled 'jack' or 'jacket'.

jazz is of uncertain origin, but is certainly from a North American source. It is considered possible that it came from Chas (a shortening of Charles), the name of a Black musician.

jeans comes from the name of the fabric used, and is short for 'jean fustian'. It was formerly spelled 'jenes' or 'geanes', from *Gênes*, a French spelling of the city of Genoa which is where the cloth was first made.

jeopardy takes its name from chess, and refers to a divided game – one for which the outcome cannot be foreseen and is therefore uncertain. The Spanish expression for this is *juego de partido* and in French *jeu parti*. The English word comes from this.

jockey is a pet form of the name Jock, which is a Scottish variety of the name Jack. In the 16th century the word jockey meant simply 'lad', but later it came to mean a 'horse-dealer' and then a 'horse-rider'.

jubilee is of Hebrew origin, and refers to a year of celebration kept every 50 years. The word comes from *yobel*, a 'ram's horn'. This is because jubilee year was proclaimed by blowing upon a ram's horn.

jumper comes from the word 'jump', which had nothing to do with leaping up and down. It meant a man's short coat or a woman's bodice, and came from an Arabic word meaning a garment such as a skirt.

ketchup is a word of Malay or Chinese origin. It is certainly from the Far East, since the word in Malay is *kechap*, and in Amoy Chinese it is *ke-tsiap* meaning a 'sauce of fish'. It reached English through Dutch.

JUMPER

ORIGINS

kidnap comes from the slang word for a child 'kid', and 'nap' an earlier form of 'nab'. It was originally used in the United States to describe someone who stole children to provide cheap labourers and servants for the plantations.

kite is an old English word and comes from the Anglo-Saxon *cyta*, which is the name of a bird of prey.

knickers is an abbreviation taken from the name Diedrich Knickerbocker, the supposed author of Washington Irving's *History of New York*. The illustrations showed characters wearing baggy knee-breeches which became known as 'knickerbockers'.

lacrosse is a French word which came into English through the French settlers in North America. The full name of the game is *le jeu de la crosse*, meaning 'the game of the crooked stick'. The word *crosse* probably comes from the German, meaning 'crutch'.

launch The word for a type of boat, comes from a quite different source from the verb 'to launch'. A launch derives from the Portuguese, who took it from the Malayan word *lanchar*, meaning 'quick' or 'nimble'. The second meaning 'to launch' comes from the word 'lance' which is a kind of spear.

ledger originally meant a book which lies permanently in one place. The word comes from an Old English root, meaning 'lay' or 'lie'.

lens takes its name from the lentil vegetable, for which the Latin name is *lens*. The reason for this is that the curved glass of a lens is shaped something like a lentil. It was first used in the 17th century.

lettuce comes from the French word *laitue*, which in turn is taken from the Latin *lactuca*. The *lact* part of the word means 'milk', used because of the milky juice of the plant.

library comes from the Latin word *libraria*, meaning a bookseller's shop. The French still use the word *librairie* in the same way.

linoleum was a trade name for a patent taken out by F. Walton in 1860 for a floor covering using linen (flax) and oil. The word is a compound of the Latin words *linum* 'flax' and *oleum* 'oil'.

lobster comes from the Anglo-Saxon word *loppestre*. This comes either from *loppe* meaning 'spider' or from the earlier word *lopust*, which by some mispronunciation comes from the Latin *locusta* meaning 'locust'.

locomotive was first used in the 17th century. It was taken from the Latin phrase *in loco moveri* 'to move by change of position in space'.

ludo is simply the Latin for 'I play', the game being a modification of the old Persian game of Pachesi, introduced into Britain in 1896.

lunch is not a shortening of 'luncheon'. In fact, the second word is a lengthening of the first. The idea was based on the English dialect word 'nuncheon', meaning 'a draught taken at noon'.

ORIGINS

M

magazine is from an Arabic word *makhazin* which is the plural form of the word *makhzan*, meaning 'storehouse'. This word describes a place where guns and arms are stored, and a receptacle for bullets. In the 17th century the word was used to mean a 'storehouse of information', leading to its present meaning.

magnolia is a flower named after Pierre Magnol (1638–1715) who was professor of botany at Montpellier, France.

malaria was once believed to have been caused by the 'bad air' given off in marshy places. It was therefore named in Italy as *mal'aria*, the short form of *mala aria*, meaning 'bad air'.

map is taken from the Latin expression *mappa mundi*, meaning 'sheet of the world'. In classical Latin, the word *mappa* meant 'table-cloth'.

margarine was invented in about 1860 by the French chemist Mèges-Mouriès. He believed that his product consisted mainly of margaric acid, discovered earlier by Chevreul. The acid formed globules like pearls, and the name was taken from the Greek *margarites* 'pearl'.

mascot comes from the Italian word *masca* 'witch'. In the form *mascotto* 'little witch', it passed into other languages, reaching English through the French *mascotte*, by which time it had begun to mean a 'good luck charm'.

mayonnaise takes its name from the capital of Minorca, Port Mahón. The sauce was named *mahonnaise* in honour of the capture of the town from the English by the French Duc de Richelieu in 1756.

mesmerize is named after one of the earliest people to practise hypnotism, the Austrian physician Friedrich Anton Mesmer (1733–1815).

migraine is the French form of the older word *megrim*, which is taken from the Greek *hemikrania* 'half-skull', because the illness affects only one side of the head.

minaret is from the Spanish word *minarete*. This in turn was taken from the Turkish word *minare*, which again came from the Arabic *manarat*. Even this word comes from another Arabic word, *manar* meaning 'lighthouse'. The final part of this word *nar* means 'fire'.

mob is an abbreviation of 'mobile', taken from the Latin expression *mobile vulgus* 'the excitable or fickle crowd'. It began as a slang expression in the 17th century, and was gradually adopted into standard English.

ORIGINS

money comes from the temple of the goddess Juno in Rome which was called Moneta – one of Juno's other titles. The Roman mint was housed in a building adjoining this temple, and the mint became known as the *moneta*. From this word came the English words 'money' and 'mint'.

monster originally meant a misshapen creature, not necessarily a large one. By the 16th century it also meant something large. The word comes from the Latin *monstrum*, meaning 'something marvellous or wonderful'.

mosquito is a Spanish and Portuguese word and means simply 'little fly'. This comes from the Latin word *musca* 'fly'.

moustache came into English from French, but other languages have a similar word, for example the Italian *mostaccio* and Spanish *mostacho*. All these come from the Greek word *mastax*, meaning 'jaw'.

mummy came to English through French and Spanish, but its origin is the Arabic word *mumiya*, meaning 'an embalmed body'. *Mum* is the Arabic word for the wax used in the preserving process.

navy is a word of Latin origin, from *navis* 'a ship'.

newt is a word changed by being mispronounced. It was originally *ewt*, and when referred to as 'an ewt' confusion led to the 'n' being tacked onto the second word. 'Ewt' comes from the early words 'evet' and 'eft', from the Anglo-Saxon *efete*.

nightingale means 'singer of the night', and is taken from the Anglo-Saxon word *nihtegale*. *Niht* means 'night' and *gale* is 'singer'.

nostalgia comes from the Greek *nostos* 'return home' and *algos* 'pain'. Together they produce the meaning of 'homesickness'.

oboe comes from the French word *hautbois*, which has the same meaning. The French word is pronounced *oh-bwah*, and the English word is an imitation of this.

ocean comes into English from the Old French word *occean*, taken from the Greek *okeanos*. This word was used to describe the 'great river' which was believed to encircle the world. The names of the present oceans have been formed in various ways. The Atlantic Ocean takes its name from Atlas, the Titan in Greek mythology who was believed to hold up the pillars of the universe. The Mediterranean (strictly, of course, a sea) is the English form of the Latin *Mare Mediterraneum* which means 'sea in the centre of the land'. The Pacific Ocean was named *Mare Pacificum* by the Portuguese explorer Magellan, because he found it peaceful and free of storms. The Arctic Ocean derives its name from its northern position. The North, or Pole Star, is in the constellation of the Great Bear, and so is called *arktos* in Greek, meaning 'bear'. 'Antarctic' simply means 'opposite to the Arctic'.

ORIGINS

ogre comes from the French, and is found in the *Fairy Stories* of Perrault, published in 1697. The word is found nowhere else and it is possible that Perrault himself invented it, although there is a Latin word *orcus*, meaning 'infernal deity'.

oratorio is the Italian form of the word 'oratory', a place of prayer. In the 16th century musical performances were held at the oratory of St Philip Neri in Rome, and so the Italian word *oratorio* was applied to all such performances.

ounce comes from the Latin *uncia* which means a twelfth part of a pound, or the twelfth part of an inch. (In troy weight, there are 12 ounces to a pound.) The word 'inch' also comes from the same Latin word.

ozone comes from the Greek *ozein*, meaning 'smell'. It was named by the scientist C.F. Schonbein in 1840 because of its peculiar smell.

pagoda comes from the Persian word *butkada*. *But* means 'idol' or 'god', and *kada* is a 'house' or 'habitation'. The whole word has the meaning 'idol-house'.

pal comes from the gypsy word *pral* or *phral* meaning 'brother'. The gypsies came from India, and the ancient Indian language, Sanskrit, also has the word *bhratri* meaning 'brother'.

pants is an abbreviation of the word 'pantaloons'. This word comes from the Italian *pantalone*, which was the name used for a stock Venetian comedy character who always wore baggy trousers.

paper comes from the French *papier* which, in turn, is taken from the Latin *papyros* and the Greek *papyrus* – the reed-like plant originally used by the Ancient Egyptians for writing on.

parakeet comes from the Spanish *periquito* and the Old French, *paroquet* also meaning 'parrot'.

pawn The two meanings of this word come from quite separate sources. The name of the chess piece comes through French from the Spanish *peon* and Italian *pedone* 'footman', and originally from the Persian *piyadah* 'foot soldier'. The meaning 'pawn' as 'something held as security' also comes from Old French; *pan* meaning 'pledge' or 'plunder'.

ORIGINS

PORPOISE OR PIG-FISH

pea is an example of a word formed from a 'false plural'. The word was originally 'pease', but people thought that it was a plural, and the ending was dropped to form *pea*. The old word is still in use in such expressions as 'pease pudding'. It is derived from the Latin word *piza*, in turn from Greek *pison*.

pepper is a word which goes right back to the ancient Sanskrit language, where it appears as *pippali*. It appears in most European languages with slightly different spellings: *pfeffer* (German), *poivre* (French) and *piper* (Latin).

petrol is the shorter form of the word 'petroleum', formed from the Latin *petra oleum*, meaning 'rock oil'.

piano is an abbreviation of *pianoforte*, which is an Italian word coming from the phrase *gravecembalo di piano e forte*, meaning 'harpsichord with soft and loud'. This description was used by the inventor Bartolomeo Cristofori in about 1710.

pilot reached English from the French *pilote*, through the Medieval Latin word *pilotus*. This in turn was taken from the Greek *pedon*, which means 'an oar' or 'a rudder'.

plagiarize originally described something far worse than its present meaning. Plagiary was kidnapping, and the word comes from the Latin *plagium* meaning 'man-stealing'.

plebiscite is of Latin origin, the first part referring to the *plebs*, who were the common people of Rome. The ending is formed from *scitum*, meaning 'law'. So the whole word refers to a law made by the common people.

pluck In modern slang English, people are referred to as having 'guts', meaning they are courageous. 'Pluck' has a similar origin. It is the act of plucking out the heart, liver and lungs from the carcass of an animal. The meaning 'to pull out' comes from the Anglo-Saxon word *pluccian*.

poker The name of the game, poker, entered English in the United States from the German *pochspiel*, which was a 'bluffing' card-game. The German word *pochen* means 'to brag or to thrust'.

porpoise comes from the Latin *porcus* 'pig' and *piscis* 'fish', suggesting that the animal is a 'pig-fish'; not true zoologically, but a fairly apt description.

ORIGINS

portcullis comes from the Old French *port coleïce*. The first word means 'door', while the second means 'sliding or gliding'.

pound comes from the Latin word *pondo*, which is the source of the meanings in English referring to weight and money. There was originally a pound weight of silver in the English pound.

pram is short for 'perambulator'. The word perambulate means 'to walk' or 'to travel', and comes from a similar Latin word. A perambulator was once a person who travelled, but was first used to describe a baby-carriage in the 19th century.

precipice once meant a 'headlong fall', but by the 17th century it had taken on its present meaning. It comes from the Latin *praecipitium*, formed from *praeceps* 'headlong, steep'.

prestige comes from the French, and originally from the Latin *praestigium*, meaning 'illusion'. It referred to the tricks used by a juggler, and 'prestigitation' still means 'performing conjuring tricks'. The modern meaning suggests 'brilliance or glamour from past successes'.

problem is from the French *problème*, taken from the Latin *problema*. This is directly from the Greek, formed from *proballein*. *Pro* means 'before, earlier' and *ballein* 'throw'.

propaganda is a word taken from the Church, and originally meant a committee of cardinals charged with foreign missions. It comes from the Latin *propagare* 'to mulitiply specimens' (such as a plant), or 'to increase or spread'.

pterodactyl is a recent word made up from Greek roots. *Pteron* means 'wing' and *daktulos* is 'finger'. This reptile's wings are formed from an extension of the front claws or 'fingers'.

pulpit comes from the Latin *pulpitum*, meaning 'a raised structure, stage or scaffold'. The French word for 'desk' *pupitre* comes from the same source.

pygmy is a word of Greek origin. The original word was *pugmaios*, meaning 'dwarfish' or 'very small'. It is taken from another Greek word *pugme* 'fist' which is also a measure of length, from the elbow to the knuckles.

quarantine is from the Medieval Latin *quadrantena*, and refers to a period of 40 days. Originally it was the legal period that a widow was allowed to remain in her late husband's house, but the present meaning came into use in about the 17th century.

quicksilver means 'living silver', from the fact that the metal runs when poured. This uses an old meaning of 'quick', in the sense of 'live'.

raisin Although it means 'a dried grape' in English, this word in some other languages simply means 'grape'. It comes from the Latin *racemus* 'a cluster of grapes'.

ORIGINS

ramshackle was once spelled and pronounced 'ranshackle', since it was a variation of the word 'ransack'. 'Ransack' comes from an Old Norse word *rannsaka*, meaning 'to search for stolen goods'. *Rann* means 'house' and *saka* means 'seek'.

rebel comes from the French *rebelle* and Latin *rebellis*. This comes from *re* 'again', and *bellum* 'war'. The word 'revel' comes from the same source, originally meaning 'to rejoice noisily' and 'to make a disturbance'.

reckless is formed from the words 'reck' and 'less'. 'Reck' means 'to take care, heed, or concern oneself'. It is an Anglo-Saxon word, spelled 'reccan'. 'Reckless' appears in Dutch as *roekeloos* and German as *ruchlos*.

reindeer is an Old Norse word, *hreindyri*, and it is from this that the English word is derived. The word appears in other European languages in different spellings: *rendier* (Dutch), *renntier* (German) or simply *renne* (French).

repair comes from the French *réparer*, and in turn from the Latin *reparare*. This uses the prefix *re* 'go back to an earlier state', plus *parare* 'to make ready, or put in order'.

republic comes from two Latin words, *res* 'affair or thing' and *publica* 'public'. The word originally was *respublica*, but the 's' was dropped in French, which is the source of the English word.

restaurant is a French word taken from the verb *restaurer* 'to restore', and the word was originally used to mean 'a food which restores'. The modern use comes from an eating-house called a *restaurant* which opened in Paris in 1765.

rhinoceros comes from the Greek *rhin-* 'nose' and *keras* 'horn', forming into a word meaning 'nose-horn'. There have been several ways of making a plural of the word ('rhinocerotes', 'rhinocerons', 'rhinocerontes'), but nowadays the correct plural is 'rhinoceroses'.

robot comes from the Czech word *robota* meaning 'compulsory service', but first acquired its modern meaning when Karel Čapek used it to mean 'mechanical slave' in his play *R.U.R.* in 1921. In Russian (a language related to Czech), the word *rabota* means 'work, labour'.

ROBOT OR MECHANICAL SLAVE

159

rosemary was, until about the 14th century, known as *rosmarine*, a word which comes from the Latin *ros marinus* meaning 'sea-dew'.

ruffian has nothing to do with the word 'rough', but comes from the Italian word *ruffiano*, taken from an older word *roffia* 'beastly thing'.

salary is from the Latin *salarium*, in turn from the word *sal* 'salt'. This is because a salary was originally money given to Roman soldiers to buy salt. Later it came to mean any kind of pay.

sandwich is a word taken from a name. John Montagu, the 11th Earl of Sandwich (1718–92), was so fond of gambling that he was reluctant to get up from the table for a meal. Instead he asked for meat to be served between two slices of bread.

sarcophagus is from the Greek *sarko* 'flesh' and *phagos* 'eating', meaning 'flesh-eating'. This was because the Ancient Greeks believed that the stone used could actually swallow up the corpse and the wooden coffin.

saucer was originally simply a small dish on which sauce was served. The word 'sauce' comes from the Latin *salsa*, meaning 'salted'. The same article is called *soucoupe* in French and *sottocoppa* in Italian, both meaning 'an under-cup'.

saxophone is named after Adolphe Sax, a Belgian who invented the instrument in 1842. He also invented the saxhorn and the saxotromba.

ADOLPHE SAX

scarlet was originally the name of a rich cloth, which was often bright red, but could also be various other colours. English took it from the Old French *escarlate* or Italian *scarlatto*. In turn, these words come from the Persian word *saqirlat* 'broadcloth'.

schooner is a word from North America. The word was sometimes spelled 'scooner', and was applied to a ship first built at Gloucester, Massachusetts in about 1713. It is probably derived from the verb 'to scon' meaning 'to send skimming over the water'.

scout originally meant 'to spy', and comes from the Old French word *escouter* 'to listen'. The Latin form is *auscultare*. So 'a scout' is someone sent out to spy or reconnoitre.

seal, in the sense of a closure, comes from the Old French *seel*, in turn taken from the Latin *sigillum* meaning 'a small picture' as well as 'seal'. The name of the animal comes from the Anglo-Saxon *seolh*.

ORIGINS

semaphore is from Greek *sema* 'signal' and *phoros* 'bearing', a word invented in about 1812 in France, and adopted into English.

sentry is a corruption of the word 'sanctuary'. This was a place of safety, and was later applied to a shelter for a watchman, and then to the watchman himself.

shack is a word from Central America and comes from the Mexican *jacal*, and in turn from the Aztec word *xacatli*, meaning a 'wooden hut'.

shanty has a similar meaning to 'shack' and comes from North America. It is a corruption of the French word *chantier*, meaning 'a workshop'. In North America it had the special meaning of 'a hut used by woodcutters'.

shawl is a word of Eastern origin. In Persian the word is *shal*, and similar words are found in Indian languages. With varying spellings the word is found in most European languages.

sheriff is an old English word, coming from the Anglo-Saxon *scirgerefa*, or 'shire-reeve'. 'Shire' refers to a county and 'reeve' was a local official.

shilling is a word found in most European languages, yet its origin is uncertain. In German it is *schilling*, in Norwegian *skilling*, in Old French and Spanish *escalin*, and in Italian *scellino*.

shirt comes from the same source as 'skirt', which is the Old Norse word *skyrta* 'shirt'. Exactly how this word came to mean two different things is not clear. In German there is another similar word *schürze*, meaning 'apron'.

shuffle comes from the German *schuffeln*, and is connected with such

ETIENNE DE SILHOUETTE

words as 'scuffle' and 'shove', all with the meaning of pushing along, putting together, or thrusting.

silhouette is named after a French politician, Etienne de Silhouette (1704–67), who is said to have been so mean that in his home he would not have fully-executed drawings, but only outlines, in order to save money.

sinister comes from the Latin, and simply means 'left' or 'to the left'. The left was associated with bad omens, while the right was favoured. The Latin word for 'right' is *dexter*, giving rise to the English 'dexterity', meaning 'skill or adroitness'.

sir is a short form of sire, a word used for people of rank. It comes from the French which, in earlier times, had *sieur*, from *seigneur*. This came from Latin *senior*. More complicated forms are *monseigneur* and *monsieur* 'my sir'. Italian also has the word *monsignor*.

ORIGINS

skipper is from the Dutch *schipper*, from the word *schip* 'ship'. The English word 'equip' is from the same source. In early France the word for 'boarding ship' was taken from the Dutch, becoming *eskip* or *esquip*. The 's' was dropped, forming the word 'equip' which has, over the years, changed its meaning.

slave comes from the Latin word *Sclavus*, meaning 'Slav', one of the peoples of Eastern Europe, such as the Russians, the Poles or Bulgarians. They had been conquered and made to serve as slaves, so the word became adapted to mean any person owned by another.

slot is of Germanic origin, and is still found in German as *schloss*, meaning 'lock', 'clasp' or 'castle'. Its original meaning in English was 'bar' or 'rod' rather than 'an opening', since it was used for bolting or locking.

smart was once used only in the sense of a sharp, stinging pain. It had the same meaning in Old English, and only in the 12th century did it come to mean 'brisk, vigorous', and later still 'clever'. The meaning of 'well-dressed' dates from the early 18th century.

smug originally meant 'trim', 'neat' or 'smooth'. From 'sleek' the meaning changed in the 19th century to 'self-satisfied'. It is probably related to the German word *schmücken* 'to adorn'.

sock originally meant 'shoe' or 'light slipper', coming from the Latin word *soccus*. Later it meant any covering for the foot and then came to mean, as it does today, a short stocking.

soldier strictly means 'someone serving in an army for pay', since the word has its origins in the Latin word *solidus* 'a gold coin'. This word changed as it was used in Portuguese and Spanish into *sueldo* and *soldo*, both names of coins and also the word for 'pay'. So a soldier was one who was paid in such coins. In France, the five-centime coin was called *sou*.

soybean is a combination of 'soya' and 'bean'. 'Soya' comes to English from the Dutch form *soja* taken from Malay *soi*. This came from the Japanese *sho-yu* and Chinese *shi-yau*, formed from *shi* 'salted beans' and *yu* 'oil'.

spaghetti is an Italian word, formed as a plural of *spaghetto*. This is taken from the word *spago*, meaning 'cord'. So the whole word means 'little cords'.

spell originally comes from a Germanic word meaning 'magic formula' and is still used in that sense. But it was also borrowed by the French, who used it to mean 'explain', and later to 'spell' words.

spider was *spithre* in Anglo-Saxon, where it had the meaning of 'spinner'. In fact, early forms of English did refer to the spider as 'spinner'.

spinach comes from the Latin word *spina*, since some varieties of the plant have prickly seeds. But it is possible that the Latin word was taken from a Persian name for spinach, *aspanakh*.

sport is an English word which has been adopted by many other languages in the world. It comes from the verb disport 'to divert, play or frolic', and originally meant any kind of pleasant pastime.

squat comes from the Old French *esquatir* 'to press flat'. Later the word changed to *quatir*, and in the form *se*

ORIGINS

MAN AND SUPERMAN

quatir meant 'to crouch'. It came into English in the 15th century.

star is of Anglo-Saxon origin, but the same root exists in many European languages. The Latin word was *stella* (from which comes the English word 'stellar'), and the Greek was *aster* (from which comes the English words 'asteroid' and 'astronaut'). In German it is *stern*, and in Italian *stella*.

steeple comes from the Anglo-Saxon *stepel* 'a tall tower', and is related to the word 'steep'. A horse-race known as a steeplechase is so called because originally the riders used a distant steeple as a landmark and goal.

sterling originally referred to a silver penny used in England in Norman times. It seems likely that the word arose from Anglo-Saxon *steorling*, from *steorra* 'star', since some of the early pennies were marked with a star. A 'pound sterling' was a pound weight of sterlings.

storey is of the same origin as 'story', and comes from the Latin word *historia* 'story, history'. *Historia* also meant 'picture' in England in the Middle Ages and it is likely that the meaning of 'storey' came about because of rows of painted windows on houses.

strand may be derived either from the Old French word *estran* 'rope', or Germanic *strang* 'rope, string'. Strand also has the meaning of 'land by the sea or water'.

street is from the Anglo-Saxon *straet*, and in turn from the Latin *strata* 'something thrown or laid down'. Languages related to English also have a similar word. In Dutch it is *straat*, and in German *strasse*.

stupid is from the Latin word *stupidus*, taken from the verb *stupere* 'to be amazed'. At one time, the word meant 'stunned with surprise', but took on its present meaning during the 16th century. 'Stupendous' is a similar word, but used in the original sense.

sugar comes from the Arabic *sukkar*, related to the Persian word *shakar* and the Greek word *sakchar*.

superman was not invented by those who devised the comic strip. In fact, the word was first used in English in 1903 by George Bernard Shaw for his play *Man and Superman*. It was an attempt to translate the German word *übermensch* used by the German writer Nietzsche. *Über* means 'over' and *mensch* is 'human being'.

163

ORIGINS

swank is a dialect word first used in the English Midlands, becoming widely known throughout the English-speaking world during this century. It might come from the German *swanken* 'to sway', or be connected to the word 'swagger'.

swastika comes from the Sanskrit *svastika*, from *svasti*, meaning 'well-being, fortune'. The symbol is also called the 'fylfot' or 'gammadion'. It later became associated with the Nazi party in Germany, although the symbol is not German.

swindle is formed from swindler, 'a cheat', and comes from the German *schwindler*. This word was brought to England by German-Jewish immigrants in the 18th century. It originally applied to someone who cadged or begged.

syrup reached English from the French word *sirop*, but it came originally from the Arabic *sharab*, from *shariba* 'to drink'. These Arabic words were also the source of our word 'sherbet'.

tabernacle and **tavern** both come from the Latin word *tabernaculum*, which meant a 'tent, booth or shed'. It was derived from another Latin word *taberna*, meaning a 'hut or booth'. Both words were adapted in French, and then taken into English.

tambourine is taken from the French *tambourin*, and earlier *tambour* and *tabour*. This referred to a small drum. This word is found in Arabic as *tambur* 'lute', and in Persian as *taburak* 'drum'.

tank As a name for the armoured fighting vehicle, this word is of British origin. It was originally used during World War I as a secret code-name for the new vehicle. When the armoured vehicle came into use, the code-name 'tank' was kept. Its original meaning for 'cistern' comes from an Indian word *tankh* 'a reservoir'.

ORIGINS

tarantula is taken from the town of Taranto, in Italy, where the spider is found.

tea is a word originally found in Amoy Chinese as *t'e*. It was adopted by the Dutch as *thee*, and so passed into European languages pronounced more or less as in English. The Mandarin Chinese word for 'tea' is *ch'a*, and so the Russians and Portuguese say *chai* or *cha*.

tennis comes from the French *tenez*, from *tenir* 'to hold'. In early times, the server shouted *tenes* to attract his or her opponent's attention.

terracotta is Italian, and literally means 'cooked earth'. The English use of the word to describe brownish-red unglazed pottery dates from the 18th century.

thesaurus is from the Greek word *thesauros*, meaning 'treasury', and was used in the early 19th century especially to describe a treasury of knowledge, or a treasury of words.

thug is from an Indian word *thag*, meaning a professional robber or murderer. It passed into English after it was used by the British army in India, and during the 19th century came to describe any cut-throat or ruffian.

ticket comes from the French word *étiquet*, formerly *estiquet* 'etiquette'. The French word came from the Old French verb *estiquer* 'to stick', which is from the German *stechen* with the same meaning.

tinsel is from the French word *étincelle* 'spark', which in turn is derived from the Latin *stincilla*.

tram once meant the shaft of a barrow

TARANTULA

or cart, and later applied to a kind of sledge or truck pulled along. The word 'tram' came to be applied to the track (made of wood, iron or stone) along which the trucks were pulled. When passenger vehicles were run on such tracks, they were called tramcars and this was later shortened to 'trams'.

treacle comes from the French *triacle*, a kind of salve or ointment used as an antidote to animal bites. Later it meant any kind of remedy, often in the form of a syrup. The word comes from Greek *theriake*, from *therion* 'wild beast' or 'poisonous animal'.

trinket originally meant a shoemaker's knife, and also had the meaning of a 'toy-knife' made especially for ladies to wear as ornaments on chains. It originates from the Old French *trenquer* 'to cut'.

ORIGINS

truant once had the meaning of 'beggar, or idle rogue', but in the 16th century it took on the meaning of a pupil absent from school. It is originally a Celtic word, and is also related to the Welsh word *truan* and Gaelic *truaghan* 'wretched'.

tsar (or **czar**) is a Russian word derived from the Latin *Caesar*. It also appears in German as *kaiser*.

turban comes to English from Portuguese *turbante*. Its origin is in the Persian word *dulband*, with the 'd' altered to a 't' and the 'l' changed to an 'r'. The English word 'tulip' also comes from the same Persian word. The Turks called the flower *tuliband*, because the shape of a turban looked like the tulip.

typhoon seems to have had several separate origins which led to one word. One was the Chinese *tai fung* 'big wind'. The other was the Arabic *tufan* 'hurricane'. Greek also had *typhon* 'whirlwind'. Originally, the words cannot have been connected, so their similar meanings are a remarkable coincidence.

umbrella is from the early Italian word *ombrella*, which meant 'little shade', since the umbrella was originally used as a sunshade. It comes from the Latin word *umbra*, meaning 'shade'.

union, **unique**, **unit** and **unite** are all from the same source, the Latin *unus* 'one'. 'Unique' is derived from Latin *unicus* 'one and only', and 'unite' from the verb *unire* 'to join together'.

urchin once meant simply 'hedgehog'. In earlier times it was also used as a slang word for 'goblin' or 'small boy or brat'. It comes from the Old French *heriçon*, from Latin *ericius* 'hedgehog'.

vaccinate comes from Latin *vacca* 'a cow'. This is because Edward Jenner invented vaccination in 1798, after he noticed that people who had suffered from cowpox were unlikely to catch smallpox. The milder disease gave the sufferer immunity against the more dangerous one; vaccination worked in the same way.

vandal The Vandals were a German tribe that invaded Western Europe in the fourth and fifth centuries AD destroying many beautiful cities and objects. After its use in the 18th century by the French revolutionary, Henri Grégoire, destructive people became known as 'vandals'.

vermin has its origins in the Latin *verminum*, from *vermis* 'worm'. Originally it meant 'worms', but later came to be used of any unwanted animals.

vicinity comes from the Latin word *vicinitas*, in turn taken from *vicinus* 'neighbour' and *vicus* 'village'. The English suffix 'wick' in place-names comes from the same source.

Viking comes from the same source as 'vicinity', since the word is based on *vik* or *wic*, meaning a camp or village. The Vikings would make temporary camps whenever they made raids in other countries.

ORIGINS

vitamin is an invented word, first used by the Polish-born American biochemist, Casimir Funk, in 1913. It is taken from Latin *vita* 'life', and the chemical *amine* (from ammonia).

volt is taken from the name of the Italian physicist and chemist, Alessandro Volta, and first came into use in 1827.

wafer originally meant a small flat cake with a honeycomb design. It is connected with the German word *wabe* 'honeycomb', but is also related to the English word 'weave'. From the same source comes the American word *waffle*.

water is a word which is found in many European languages with different spellings and varying pronunciation. In Dutch it is *water*, German has *wasser*, and in Russian it takes the form *voda*.

web once meant 'woven fabric' and can still be used in that sense. In the 13th century it was also used to mean 'cobweb' or 'tissue'.

Welsh is from the Old English word *waelisc*, meaning 'foreign'. It originates in the name of a Celtic tribe, known in Latin as the *Volcae*. It is the second part of the name 'Cornwall', and is found too in the name of the French-speaking Belgians, the 'Walloons'.

wigwam is taken from a North American Indian word. This word varies from tribe to tribe, as *wikiwam*, *weekuwom* or *wiquoam*, and means 'their house'.

window comes from the Early English word *windoge*, from the Old Norse word *vindauga* meaning 'wind-eye'. An early name in Anglo-Saxon times was *eagdura* 'eye-door'.

wistaria This plant was named in honour of the American anatomist Caspar Wistar (1761–1818).

worm has not always meant 'earthworm'. It was originally used to describe dragons and serpents. It comes from a Germanic root, but is related to Greek *rhomos* 'woodworm' and Latin *vermis* 'worm'.

ORIGINS

wrong originally meant 'crooked, twisted or bent'. In Anglo-Saxon, the word was *wrang* meaning 'injustice'. It took on the meaning of 'incorrect' in about the 13th century.

yoga is a Hindi word meaning 'union with the Supreme Spirit', and is taken from a similar word in Sanskrit, meaning 'union'. A 'yogi' is one who practises meditation.

xylophone takes its name from two Greek words, *xylo* 'wood' and *phonos* 'sound'. This is because the instrument is made of flat wooden bars.

zany is from the Italian *zanni*, which is simply a dialect form of the name 'John' – *Giovanni*. A zany was originally a kind of comic performer; a sort of clown's assistant. Later it was used to mean a simpleton or idiot.

zest originally had the meaning of orange or lemon peel used as a flavouring and it still retains that meaning. Its other meaning of 'relish' or 'gusto' came into use during the 18th century. The word comes from the French *zeste*.

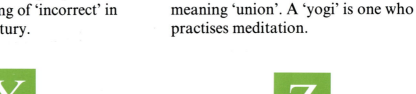

Yiddish is taken from the German word *jüdisch*, which means 'Jewish'. In German, the word is pronounced very much as it is spelled in English.

ENGLISH USAGE

ENGLISH USAGE

Although English grammar is not as difficult as the grammar of many other European languages, English does present some difficulties, and even good speakers and writers are sometimes inclined to make mistakes. For example, you hear on radio or television someone telling you that 'we need less people to work in factories or offices'. This is wrong. What should have been said was 'we need *fewer* people'. The word 'people' refers not to a substance, such as sugar, but to separate things. This listing will warn you of a few of the pitfalls in English, and help you to overcome them.

a, an The indefinite article. *A* is used before a noun which starts with a consonant, as in *a book, a ship, a building*; while *an* is used before a noun which starts with a vowel, as in *an earwig, an egg, an article*. Before words beginning with a silent *h*, the word *an* is used, as in *an honour, an hour, an heir*.

abbreviations Shortened forms of words and phrases (*see box*).

-able, -ible These suffixes can be added to certain verbs and nouns to form adjectives. Examples of the *-able* suffix are: *bearable, readable, reliable, passable*. If the suffix *-able* is added to words ending in *e*, the *e* is usually dropped, but there are some words which can be spelled both ways, for example: *blamable* or *blameable, likable* or *likeable, livable* or *liveable, sizable* or *sizeable, unshakable* or *unshakeable*. Examples of words with the *-ible* suffix are: *accessible, audible, collapsible, compatible, credible, digestible, divisible, edible, eligible, fallible, flexible, indelible, intelligible, possible, visible*.

above and **over** The first word means 'at a higher level than', and the second word means 'on top of'. Sometimes both can mean the same thing, for example: 'Mr and Mrs Singh lived *over* [or *above*] the shop'.

abbreviations	
a.m.	before noon (*ante meridiem*)
BA	Bachelor of Arts
BSc	Bachelor of Sciences
cm	centimetre(s)
Dr	doctor
etc.	and so on (*et cetera*)
GB	Great Britain
kg	kilogramme(s)
kph	kilometres per hour
l	litre(s)
m	metre(s)
mph	miles per hour
Mr	Mister
Mrs	Mistress
NB	take note (*nota bene*)
p	page
p.m.	after noon (*post meridiem*)
pp	pages
rpm	revolutions per minute
RSVP	please reply (*répondez s'il vous plaît*)
sae	stamped addressed envelope
UK	United Kingdom
USA	United States of America
v	against (*versus*)

ENGLISH USAGE

abstract and concrete Abstract nouns are names of things which cannot be touched, but only thought about. Concrete nouns are actual things which exist. Examples of abstract nouns are: *fear, anger, speed, freedom, happiness, patience, honesty*. The following are examples of concrete nouns: *box, railway, school, girl, country*; in fact anything which you can see, touch or hear.

accent This refers to the syllable which is stressed in a word. In the following examples the stress or accent is shown by printing the accented syllable in capital letters: *TAIlor, INsect, STORy, reQUEST, HAPpiness, aLARM, imMEDiate*. Sometimes, when a word can be used as both a noun and verb, the accent or stress changes. You set an example by good *CONduct*, but you *conDUCT* an orchestra.

accept and **except** *Accept* is a verb, and means 'to take or receive', while *except* is a preposition meaning 'other than' or 'apart from'.

acetic and **ascetic** The first word refers to *acetic* acid, which is similar to vinegar. The second word means someone who practises self-denial.

acronym A word made up of the initials, or part-syllables of a phrase (*see box*).

AD and **BC** AD stands for *Anno Domini*, Latin for 'in the year of the Lord' and BC stands for 'before Christ'. AD should be written before the year, as in 'AD 1984', while BC should be written after the year, as in '96 BC'

adjective An adjective describes things, ideas or living beings and is often used to give more information about a noun. Here are some examples of adjectives: 'That is a *fast* car', 'What a *pretty* flower!', 'I eat from a *wooden* table'. Adjectives can be formed from nouns and verbs (*see box*). Adjectives formed from proper nouns take a capital letter: *American, Swedish, Christian, Jewish*.

---

acronyms
AIDS: **a**cquired **i**mmune **d**eficiency **s**yndrome
laser: **l**ight **a**mplifications by **s**timulated **e**mission of **r**adiation
Nato: **N**orth **A**tlantic **T**reaty **O**rganization
Oxfam: **O**xford Committee for **Fam**ine Relief
radar: **ra**dio **d**etection **a**nd **r**anging
sonar: **so**und **na**vigation **r**anging
Unesco: **U**nited **N**ations **E**ducational, **S**cientific and **C**ultural **O**rganization

ENGLISH USAGE

Adjectives
formed from nouns:

acrobat	acrobatic
arch	arched
bride	bridal
character	characteristic
colour	colourful
emotion	emotional
friend	friendly
gold	golden
juice	juicy
monster	monstrous
navy	naval
picture	picturesque
reflex	reflexive
water	watery

formed from verbs:

collapse	collapsible
defend	defensive
eat	eatable
love	lovable
possess	possessive

adverse and **averse** The first word means 'unfavourable', while the second means 'unwilling, against or opposed to'. Examples are: 'He had an *adverse* report from his school', 'What boy or girl is *averse* to eating ice-cream?'.

affect and **effect** The first word is a verb, and means 'to act upon or influence', while the second word can be either a noun and mean 'the result or consequence of an action', or a verb meaning 'to bring about'. Here are some examples: 'Your advice will *affect* my decision', 'We sent Lucy to a new school, which had a good *effect* on her behaviour', 'The prisoner had *effected* his escape'.

adverbs
early
finally
never
slowly
sometimes
wearily
yesterday

admit This verb can mean two quite different things. The first meaning is 'to confess or acknowledge' a sin or crime, and the second is 'to allow to enter'.

adverb An adverb describes a verb and tells how, when or where something happens, for example: *carefully, easily, visibly, truthfully, happily*. You can say that 'Jim writes *beautifully*' or 'Hannah sings *superbly*'. These adverbs are easy to recognize because they end in 'ly'. But not all adverbs do. Here are some more examples of adverbs which tell how, when or where: 'He *always* gets cross if you argue with him', 'Ann wants you to telephone her *now*', 'I like eating *here*'.

A PRISONER EFFECTING HIS ESCAPE

ENGLISH USAGE

afflict and **inflict** The first word means 'to trouble or pain', while the second means 'to impose or enforce, or to cause suffering'. Examples are: 'My mother is badly *afflicted* by rheumatism', 'The enemy planes bombed the town, *inflicting* much loss of life'.

aggravate This word is often used to mean 'to annoy or irritate', such as in the sentence 'My little brother often *aggravates* me'. However, its proper meaning is 'to make worse', as in the sentence: 'Her bad cold was *aggravated* by the damp climate'.

alphabetical order It is sometimes useful to list items or names in *alphabetical order*. To do this, you should take each letter as it appears, ignoring spaces, hyphens and other marks, such as apostrophes.

Look first at the initial letters of the words you wish to alphabetize and arrange them in the order of the alphabet, for example: *lion* would come before *mother, water* after *vole*. If several words start with the same letter, or group of letters, look in turn at the second, third, fourth etc. letters of the word. For example, *move, mouse, moat, moan* and *more* arranged into alphabetical order give the following list *moan, moat, more, mouse, move*.

Names beginning with *Mac, Mc* or *M'* should all be regarded as if they were spelled *Mac*. The abbreviation *St* for 'Saint' should be treated as if it were spelled out: *Saint Matthew*. Similarly, names like *S. Pedro* and *S. Maria* should be treated as if the names were spelled in full: *San Pedro* and *Santa Maria*. Abbreviations such as EC, NATO or UNESCO should be treated as if they are ordinary words, and placed alphabetically as they appear.

already and **all ready** These two should not be confused. *Already* is an adverb, as used in the sentence 'The shops were *already* open by the time I reached the centre'. *All ready* is an adjectival phrase, as used in the sentence 'We were *all ready* to depart when John arrived'.

altar and **alter** The first word means a table or structure in a church, while the second means 'to change something'.

anagram An *anagram* is a word formed by using the letters of one word rearranged to form one or more other words. Here are some examples: *angle* can be rearranged to make the word *glean, pirates* can be rearranged to spell *sea trip*, and *telegraph* can be rearranged to make *great help*.

ENGLISH USAGE

anagrams	
nameless	salesmen
despair	praised
it ran	train
infection	fine tonic
punishment	nine thumps
solemn	melons
night	thing

& [and] This symbol is called an *ampersand*, and means simply *and*. However, its use should be limited to the names of firms or companies: *Henry Robinson & Co., Babcock & Wilcox*.

ante and **anti** These two prefixes mean quite different things. The first means 'before' and the second means 'against or opposed to'. An *anteroom* is a small room giving access to a larger one. *Anti-clockwise* means 'in the opposite direction to the rotation of the hands of a clock'.

antonym An antonym is a word which gives the opposite meaning to another (*see box*).

antonyms	
advance	retreat
clean	dirty
clever	stupid
covered	uncovered
deep	shallow
freedom	captivity
giant	dwarf
help	hinder
hope	despair
light	dark
low	high
obey	disobey
slow	quick
swim	sink
thick	thin
under	over
up	down

apostrophe ['] This is a punctuation mark, and is used to show contractions when letters are omitted, for example, *don't* for 'do not'. It is also used to indicate the possessive form of nouns and some pronouns, for example: *Joseph's brother, the girls' shoes, a week's holiday*.

artist and **artiste** The first word refers to someone like a painter, sculptor or musician, while the second refers to someone who works as an entertainer, such as a singer or comedian.

as *As* should not usually be used as an alternative word to *because*. For instance 'I cannot come to your party as I am going to the doctor' could mean that the writer could not come to the party *on his way* to the doctor! In this case the word *as* should be replaced by *because*.

ENGLISH USAGE

B

C

balmy and **barmy** The first of these words means 'sweet-smelling' or 'mild and pleasant'. The second is a slang word, meaning 'silly or foolish'. Although both words are sometimes spelled 'balmy', it is better to use the second spelling for the meaning 'foolish'.

because This word means 'for the reason that'. *Because* is sometimes replaced by *as* or *since*, especially at the beginning of sentences: '*As* you've come such a long way, perhaps you'd like to stay to dinner?', '*Since* you ask, I must tell you that I shall be leaving tomorrow'.

beside and **besides** *Beside* means 'by the side of', and *besides* means 'in addition' or 'moreover': 'I do like to be *beside* the seaside', 'I didn't like that house, and *besides*, it was on the wrong side of the road'.

biannual and **biennial** *Biannual* means 'twice a year', and *biennial* means 'occurring every two years'.

bizarre and **bazaar** The first word means 'odd or unusual' from the Italian *bizzarro*. The second means 'a type of market' from the Persian word for a market *bazar*.

buffet There are two words spelled in this way. The first refers to a bar or counter where food is served. In this case, the word is a French one and is pronounced *bu-fay*, while the second is pronounced *buffit* and means 'to strike or knock something'.

calendar, **calender** and **colander** A *calendar* is something which tells you the date, a *calender* is a machine which smooths cloth or paper, and a *colander* is a kitchen utensil used for draining vegetables.

can and **may** The word *can* means 'ability to do something', while *may* means 'to have permission to'. For example: '*Can* I leave school early today?' means 'am I *able* to leave school early today?'. The answer to that is, 'yes, you are *able* to do so, but you still need permission!'. The correct question is: '*May* I leave school early today?'.

ENGLISH USAGE

cancel and **postpone** *Cancel* means 'to call off completely', while *postpone* means 'to put off until another time'.

capital letters Capital letters are used in the following cases:
  For proper nouns and their adjectives: *Henry Jones, Mrs Edith Johnson, Uncle Harry, Germany, German, Bovril, the United States, American, Marxist.*
  At the beginning of a sentence: *All sentences begin with a capital letter.*
  For the names of the days of the week, months of the year and festivals: *January, Monday, Christmas Day.*
  For titles of people: *Her Majesty, Lord Williams, President Bush.*
  For the name of God: *God, Allah.*
  For the titles of books, newspapers, plays, films etc: *Charlie and the Chocolate Factory, The Great Gatsby, The Mousetrap, The Times.*

cereal and **serial** A *cereal* is a plant from which grain, such as oats, barley or wheat, is produced, while a *serial* is a story told in episodes or parts.

chord and **cord** A *chord* is a musical term which refers to sounding several notes together, while *cord* is a kind of rope or string.

clause A *clause* is a sentence which is part of a larger sentence. For instance, 'Jane spoke to Henry and Bill took Mary's arm' is one sentence, but it contains two shorter sentences or *clauses: Jane spoke to Henry* and *Bill took Mary's arm.* These two *clauses* are joined together by the word 'and' to make one sentence. *Clauses* can be linked by other words, too. In 'I was in the shop when I saw Joe', the first *clause: I was in the shop* is linked to the second *I saw Joe* by the word *when*.

clichés A *cliché* is a phrase or sentence which is so often used that it has become boring and commonplace. It is best to avoid *clichés* if you can, particularly in written work. Here are some which are often heard: *as good as gold, a blessing in disguise, explore every avenue, leave no stone unturned, the wind of change.*

coarse and **course** *Coarse* means 'rough or unrefined', while *course* means 'a track where races are held' or 'a series of lessons'.

colon [:] This is a punctuation mark. It is used to separate clauses in a sentence, when the second part explains or reveals the first. For example: 'Alison was very unhappy: she had lost her kitten', 'Tom could not get into his house: he had the wrong key'. You can also use colons to precede a list, 'I suggest you buy some vegetables: onions, potatoes and cabbage'.

comma [,] This is a punctuation mark. It is used in the following ways:
  To separate a series of things or items: 'We are going to Europe and will visit France, Germany, Italy and Spain', 'Would you like tea, coffee, milk or cocoa?'.
  Between a number of adjectives before a noun: 'What a nice, pleasant, intelligent person!', 'The film was fantastic, exciting, entertaining and full of adventure'.
  To separate clauses in a sentence: 'My friend Raji, who has dark hair, has just won a school prize', 'Jack, would you please come to my room?'.
In a list it is usual to omit the comma at the end after the last word before *and* and *or*, and before the final noun.

ENGLISH USAGE

comparatives A *comparative* is a form of an adjective or adverb which indicates 'more'. It is formed by adding *-er, -est, more* or *most*. The first form of an adjective is called the *positive*, the second is called the *comparative* and the third is called the *superlative*. Here are examples of the three, using the adjective 'quick':

'This is the quick way into town.'
 [*positive*]
'This is the quicker way into town.'
 [*comparative*]
'This is the quickest way into town.'
 [*superlative*]

You should use the *comparative* when **two** items are being discussed. In the example above, if there were only two ways into town, you would have said that one was *quicker* than the other. If there were three or more, you would have used the *superlative*.

Another example is: 'We have two guinea-pigs at home and the brown one is *the largest*'. This is wrong, since you cannot have the *largest* of two. The correct sentence should read: 'We have two guinea-pigs at home and the brown one is *the larger*'. The following sentence is correct: 'I am *the tallest* boy in my school' because it can be assumed that there are more than two boys in the school.

Sometimes, it is not possible to add *-er* or *-est* to the adjective or adverb. Take the word *beautiful*. You cannot say *beautifuler*. Instead, you should say *more beautiful*, as in: 'My sister is *more beautiful* than her cousin'. Or, for the superlative, 'My sister is the *most beautiful* girl in the family'.

competition and **contest** The word *contest* is mostly used for something which is officially organized, while *competition* is considered rather more informal. For example: 'Fred hopes to win the "best singer" *contest* next month. I expect there will be a lot of *competition* to get seats'.

complement and **compliment** The first word means 'a complete amount', while the second means 'a remark expressing admiration'. For example: 'We went to

178

ENGLISH USAGE

sea with a full *complement* of crew', 'Jenny was pleased at the *compliment* when her teacher said that her drawing was the best she had seen'.

conjunction A *conjunction* is a word which links two or more other words, clauses or sentences (*see box*). A *conjunction* can be used to join words, such as in 'bread *and* butter', 'slow *but* sure', 'ugly *yet* attractive'. Another use is to connect phrases: 'He wants to learn *but* is too lazy to try', 'Jodie likes Jon *because* he is so kind'.

continual and **continuous** The first word means 'recurring frequently, especially at regular intervals', while the second means 'unceasing, without break'. For example: '*Continuous* work is impossible if there are *continual* interruptions'.

council and **counsel** The word *council* refers to 'an assembly of people', while *counsel* means 'advice or guidance'. For example: 'The city *council* meets once a month', 'I always take *counsel* from a friend if I need help'.

curb and **kerb** The first word means 'to check or hold back', while the second refers to the edging stone of a pavement. In the United States, both words are usually spelled *curb*.

currant and **current** The first word means 'a type of dried fruit', and the second 'most recent, up-to-date' or 'a flow of water or electricity'.

conjunctions	
after	if
although	or
and	since
because	until
before	when
but	yet

contraction This is a shortening of words by combining them together with an apostrophe [']. The apostrophe shows where a letter or letters are missing. Here are some examples: I am – *I'm*; she is – *she's*; you are – *you're*; cannot – *can't*; is not – *isn't*; shall not – *shan't*.

It is important to place the apostrophe in the right position. It should indicate where the letter or letters are missing.

decimate This word is often used to mean 'to do great damage or to kill many people'. In fact, the original meaning was 'to destroy one person in ten'.

dependant and **dependent** The word *dependant* is a noun which means 'someone who depends on another person for aid', while *dependent* is an adjective and means 'depending on'. For example: 'Their *dependants* were *dependent* upon them for food and clothing'. In the United States, both words are often spelled *dependent*.

desert and **dessert** The first word means 'an arid, uncultivated place', while *dessert* is a pudding, usually the last course in a meal.

desiccate This word is frequently misspelled. It has one *s* and two *c*'s.

ENGLISH USAGE

different to, from, than *Different from* is the most usual and acceptable form of this expression, although *different to* and, in the United States, *different than* are sometimes used.

dinghy and **dingy** These two words are pronounced differently and mean different things. *Dinghy* (pronounced with a hard 'g' as in 'get') is a small boat, while *dingy* (pronounced with a soft 'g' as in 'gin') means 'drab or shabby'.

diphthong This word describes two vowels which are joined together and pronounced as one. Examples are *au, ou, ea, oi, ow, aw*. The letter *w* in these cases counts as a vowel.

discomfit and **discomfort** The word *discomfit* means 'to make uneasy or confused; to frustrate or defeat'. *Discomfort* is usually a noun and means 'inconvenience, distress or mild pain'. It can sometimes be used as a verb, when it means 'to make uncomfortable or cause distress'.

discreet and **discrete** *Discreet* means 'careful to avoid embarrassment', while *discrete* means 'separate or distinct'.

disinterested and **uninterested** These two words do not mean the same thing. *Disinterested* means 'free from bias; impartial', while *uninterested* means 'indifferent or having no interest in something; bored'.

double negative Negatives are such words as *no, not, neither, never, nothing, nobody, nowhere*. Examples of *double negatives* in sentences are: 'I *didn't* do *nothing* wrong', 'I *haven't never* been lost'. They are wrong because the two negatives cancel each other out. Correctly, the two sentences should read, 'I *did nothing* wrong', or 'I *didn't* do *anything* wrong' and 'I *have never* been lost'.

There are some instances where *double negatives* can be used correctly. 'It is *not unusual* to see a rainbow' or 'I am *not ungrateful* for your help' are both perfectly good English.

drink The past tense of *drink* is *drank*. The past participle is *drunk*. As an adjective, the word is *drunken* and sometimes *drunk*. For example: 'He *drank* some wine', 'He has *drunk* some wine', 'The soldiers were *drunk*', 'A group of *drunken* soldiers entered the town'. It would be incorrect to say 'He *drunk* the wine'.

ENGLISH USAGE

eatable and **edible** *Eatable* implies that something is not only fit to eat, but enticing, while *edible* means simply 'fit to eat without harm'.

e.g. and **i.e.** The first is an abbreviation of the Latin *exempli gratia*, which means 'for example'; while the second, again Latin, comes from *idem est*, meaning 'that is to say'. The two expressions are not interchangeable. For example: 'We have a great selection of garden flowers, *e.g.* fuchsias, roses, geraniums and lilies'. Whereas 'I expect the exhibition will attract large numbers of philatelists, *i.e.* stamp collectors'.

-ei- There is an old spelling rule which says '*i* before *e* except after *c*'. It is true in the majority of cases (*see box*), but there are a number of other words which use *ei*: *counterfeit, deign, either, feign, foreign, freight, height, kaleidoscope, leisure, neighbour, neither, reign, seize, sleigh, their* and *vein* are just a few. There are also some words in which *ie* follows *c*, for example: *ancient, glacier, science* and *species*.

-ei- words

ceiling	deceive
conceivable	perceive
conceive	receipt
deceipt	receive

---

either This word is applied to one of two persons or things. For example: 'You can have *either* tea or coffee'. *Either* is a singular word, as shown in the following sentence: '*Either* Charles or Harry *was* to be considered', not '*Either* Charles or Harry *were* to be considered'. The same rule also applies to *neither* and *nor*.

elder and **older** The word *elder* is used when you are speaking of people from the same family, such as in 'Celia is the *elder* of our two daughters'. In other circumstances, you should use *older*, as in 'My friend Celia is *older* than she looks', 'That theatre is *older* than any other building in the town'. The same rules apply to *eldest* and *oldest*.

eligible and **illegible** The word *eligible* means 'worthy or qualified'; *illegible* means 'difficult to read'.

enormity and **immensity** The word *enormity* means 'an atrocity, an act of great wickedness', as in the sentence 'The judge considered the *enormity* of the prisoner's crimes and sentenced him to a long period of imprisonment'. *Enormity* is often used incorrectly to mean 'greatness' or 'a great amount'. The correct word in this case is *immensity*, for example, 'She hadn't realized the *immensity* of the problem'.

rules are there to be broken!

ENGLISH USAGE

ensure and **insure** The first word means 'to make certain or sure', while the second means 'to guarantee or protect against risk'. In the United States both words are spelled *insure*.

eponym This is a word which is taken from someone's name (*see box*).

-ess This is a suffix which is often added to words to denote a feminine person or animal. Many of these words are rarely used, for example *authoress, conductress, editress, manageress, poetess, sculptress*. Women are now given the same titles as men: *author, conductor, editor, manager, poet,*

> **eponyms**
> boycott: Captain Boycott
> braille: Louis Braille
> leotard: Jules Léotard
> magnolia: Pierre Magnol
> maverick: Samuel Augustus Maverick
> plimsoll: Samuel Plimsoll
> teddy bear: Theodore (Teddy) Roosevelt
> sandwich: Earl of Sandwich
> shrapnel: General Shrapnel
> wellingtons: Duke of Wellington

sculptor. A few *-ess* words, such as *actress, hostess, stewardess, waitress*, remain, and the feminine form of titles such as *baroness, countess, duchess, empress, goddess, princess* are still used. Some words ending in *-ess* are male, *marquess*, for instance.

euphemisms A *euphemism* is an attempt to make something unpleasant sound less so by substituting different words. For instance, instead of saying 'she has died', you might say 'she has passed away'. Many people try to avoid saying certain words, for example using *tummy* instead of 'belly', the *smallest room* for 'toilet' or 'loo', *perspire* for 'sweat' and *stout* instead of 'fat'.

exclamation mark [!] This is a punctuation mark. It is used at the end of a sentence to express surprise, amusement, disagreement or a command. For example: 'Hooray!', 'Get out!', 'What fun!', 'Don't you dare to speak to me like that!'. It is never advisable to use too many *exclamation marks* in written work, since they will lose their impact. Never confuse an *exclamation mark* with a question mark. 'Whoever did that?' is a question, not an exclamation.

ENGLISH USAGE

faint and **feint** *Faint* has two meanings. As an adjective it means 'unclear or not bright'. As a verb it means 'to lose consciousness'. *Feint*, on the other hand, means 'a mock attack or movement'.

fantastic Although it is often used in this sense, strictly *fantastic* does not mean 'wonderful' or 'excellent'. To say 'we had a *fantastic* time in America' is incorrect if what is meant is 'we had a *great* time in America'. The word *fantastic* actually means 'strange or fanciful'.

farther and **further** If you are talking about distance, then *farther* should be used, as in 'Moscow is *farther* from London than from Berlin'. In other senses only *further* can be used, for example: 'are there any *further* questions?' or '*further* to my remarks yesterday, I have one suggestion to make'.

fatal and **fateful** *Fatal* means 'resulting in death', while *fateful* means 'having momentous consequences or controlled by fate'.

fewer and **less** *Fewer* means 'smaller in number', and *less* means 'a smaller quantity or amount'. These two words are often confused. You might hear someone say: 'We shall need *less* people to do this job' but this is incorrect because people are counted in numbers, not in quantity. The correct sentence should be: 'We shall need *fewer* people to do this job'. If you are dealing with an amount, then you should say, for instance: 'This recipe needs *less* sugar'. Again, you would be wrong in saying: 'I shall buy *less* apples this week', because apples are a number of separate things. The sentence should be: 'I shall buy *fewer* apples this week'.

figurative language can take many forms. *Figures of speech* are ways of expressing something by other means than the literal truth. You can use *irony*, which is a way of saying something when you actually mean the opposite, such as in 'you're a fine one to talk!' You can employ *paradox*, which is saying something which is apparently nonsense, but which really makes sense, such as 'make haste slowly', or 'the child is father of the man'. You can use *metaphors*, such as 'the kettle is boiling' and 'a bed of roses'. In each of these cases, you understand a meaning. You know that it is the water which is boiling, not the kettle, and that the bed of roses has nothing to do with roses at all, but describes something pleasant.

full stop/full point [.] The full stop or full point is a punctuation mark and is placed at the end of a sentence. It is also used to denote that a word is abbreviated, as in *no.* for 'number', or *Dr.* for 'doctor'. The full stop or full point is also known as the 'period', or sometimes just as a 'point'. It is now quite common for the full stop to be omitted after some abbreviations such as *Mr, Mrs, mph, anon*.

fulsome does not mean 'very full'. It means 'nauseous, excessive or insincere'. It comes from the Old English *fulsom* meaning 'copious' and 'cloying'.

ENGLISH USAGE

gender Many languages, such as French, German and Latin, have masculine and feminine nouns. In French, for example, the word for 'table' is feminine, *la table*, but 'fire' is masculine, *le feu*.

Gender does not apply in English, but there are some nouns which refer specifically to a masculine or feminine person or animal, for example: *bride, groom; goose, gander; ram, ewe; cock, hen*. There are also some nouns which change their form depending upon the gender of the subject they are naming: *actor, actress; waiter, waitress; god, goddess; prince, princess*.

Gender is also used in English pronouns: *he, him his* are the masculine forms; *she, her hers* are the feminine forms. The neuter forms, describing a thing rather than a person or animal, are *it* and *its*.

glasnost This is a Russian word which has only recently entered the English language. It means 'openness'.

gorilla and **guerilla** *Gorilla* is the name of a particular species of great apes, while *guerilla* (sometimes spelled *guerrilla*) is 'a member of an irregular army'.

gourmand and **gourmet** These two words have similar meanings, but there is one big difference. *Gourmand* is an unflattering term and means 'a glutton, or someone who likes food but eats greedily', while *gourmet* means 'someone who likes food but who is discriminating and careful as to how or what they eat'.

grill and **grille** A *grill* is a plate or bars placed above heat for cooking meat or other food. The word can also be used as a verb, *to grill*, which describes the way such food is cooked. A *grille* is a framework of metal bars over a window.

grisly, **gristly** and **grizzly** The first word, *grisly*, means 'horrible or gruesome'. *Gristly* means 'containing much gristle'. *Grizzly* means 'grey' and is applied to a particular sort of bear, the *grizzly bear*, because of its colour.

ENGLISH USAGE

hail and **hale** The word *hail* as a noun means 'frozen rain pellets'; as a verb it means 'to greet' or 'to be native to a particular country'. The word *hale* means 'healthy or robust'.

hangar and **hanger** A *hangar* is 'a building for storing aircraft', and a *hanger* is 'a support for something hanging', such as a *coat hanger*.

hiccup and **hiccough** The first word is the correct spelling, although the second is commonly used.

hoard and **horde** The first word means 'an accumulated store', and the second means 'a vast crowd'.

homonym *Homonym* comes from two Greek words meaning 'the same' and 'name'. A homonym is therefore a word which has the same sound as another, but which has a different meaning, and usually a different spelling. For instance: *right, rite, write* and *wright* all sound the same, but have quite different meanings. A word which sounds the same as another but is spelled differently is known as a *homophone* (*see box*). A word which has several different meanings is called a *homograph* for example: 'She was in the *right*', 'I told him to turn *right* at the end of the road'.

hyperbole This word, which is taken from the Greek, is pronounced 'hyPERbolee' and means 'a figure of speech which uses exaggeration to make its point'. Here are some examples of *hyperbole*: 'A thousand apologies', 'You'll die laughing when you hear this!', 'She cried her eyes out'.

homophones	
beer	bier
here	hear
lie	lye
meet	meat
scull	skull
sum	some
sun	son
there	their
wait	weight
ware	wear

hyphen Hyphens are mostly used to indicate that two or more words should be regarded as one, such as *fall-out, ice-cream, frying-pan, happy-go-lucky, good-for-nothing, stick-in-the-mud*. A hyphen is also used with certain prefixes, such as *co-* or *re-*, in words like *co-operate*, and *re-count* which means 'to count again', to avoid confusion with the word *recount* which means 'to tell a story'. A hyphen is also used in books to show where a word-break appears at the end of a line.

illegible and **unreadable** The word *illegible* is an adjective and means 'difficult to read, because it is faint or badly printed'. *Unreadable*, also an adjective, means 'badly-worded or very dull'.

inapt and **inept** The word *inapt* means 'unsuitable', while the word *inept* means 'awkward or clumsy'.

ENGLISH USAGE

incredible and **incredulous** The first word, *incredible*, means 'beyond belief or understanding', while *incredulous* means 'unwilling to believe something'.

infinitive This is the word used to describe the basic 'name' of a verb. In English, this usually takes a form starting with *to*. The following are some *infinitives* of verbs: *to walk, to ride, to eat, to sleep, to be, to go*. The word *to* is omitted when the verb follows some other, auxiliary (or helping) verbs: *I must go, we might win, you may speak, they have gone*.

If an adverb or phrase comes between the word *to* and the verb, such as in *to rarely be, to quickly eat, to in some way run, to almost always sit*, it is called a *split infinitive*. Some people regard a split infinitive as a grammatical error, but this is not the case. The famous line '*to boldly go where no man has gone before*', which comes from the TV series 'Star Trek', is another typical case of a *split infinitive*.

It is best to word a sentence in the most elegant way, whether the infinitive is split or not. In fact, there are times when it is almost impossible to write a sentence without splitting the infinitive. In the sentence, 'In my new job I hope *to more than double* my salary', the phrase 'more than' cannot be moved elsewhere in the sentence without destroying the meaning.

inflammable and **flammable** Both these words mean the same thing: 'liable to catch fire and burn easily'. It is possible to mistake the meaning of the first word for 'unlikely to burn, or non-burnable', so some people think that it is better always to use the word *flammable* to avoid confusion.

ingenious and **ingenuous** The word *ingenious* means 'skilful or clever', and the word *ingenuous* means 'naïve or innocent'.

interjection This is a term used in grammar to describe a particular type of word. *Interjections* express an exclamation and, in fact, are usually followed by an exclamation mark: '*Hooray!*', '*Alas!*', '*Oh!*'. Some *interjections* contain more than one word, such as: '*Oh, dear!*', '*Good gracious!*'. *Interjections* can be part of a sentence too: 'Fred, *alas*, was late as usual' (*see box*).

---

interjections

Hooray!	Good gracious!
Alas!	Great!
Oh!	Phew!
Ah!	Ugh!
Hey!	Well I never!
Oh dear!	

---

invite This is a verb, and means 'to ask someone politely and graciously'. The noun is *invitation* and is something you can send, or offer, by word of mouth. It is wrong to use *invite* as a noun, as in 'I'll send you an *invite*' and this should always be avoided.

its and **it's** The first word is the possessive form of the word *it*, and is used in such sentences as: 'The elephant lifted *its* trunk above *its* head'. The word *it's* is a contraction or shortening of the two words *it is*, as can be seen in the sentence: '*It's* not easy to pass examinations'. The two words are often confused, but it is wrong to use one in place of the other.

ENGLISH USAGE

THE ELEPHANT LIFTED ITS TRUNK ABOVE ITS HEAD

L

lama and **llama** A *lama* is a Buddhist monk, and a *llama* is a South American animal of the camel family.

lath and **lathe** A *lath* is a strip of wood, while a *lathe* is a machine for turning wood, metal or similar material.

lay and **lie** These are two different verbs. The problem is that the past tense of *lie* is *lay*, which is why the two verbs are sometimes confused. The verb *to lie* means 'to recline, rest or be horizontal'. The verb *to lay* means 'to put down, or to deposit, or to place'. Here are some examples of the use of the verb *to lie*: 'I am going *to lie down*', 'It is a warm day, I *shall lie* in the sun', 'Yesterday, *I lay* in bed thinking'. The word *lay* here is the past tense. Now, here are some examples of the use of the word *to lay*. 'After you finish reading, *lay* the book down', 'I'm sure I *laid* my pencil on this table yesterday'. The word *laid* here is the past tense.

There is, of course, another verb *to lie*, which means 'not to tell the truth'. In the present tense, this takes the form *lie, lies, lying*, and in the past tense *lied*, as in 'Tom is a truthful boy; he has never *lied* to me'.

learn and **teach** The confusion of these two words is fairly common. The use of *learn* in 'I go to school and Miss Jones *learns* me lessons' is wrong. The correct version should be 'I go to school and Miss Jones *teaches* me lessons'. *Learn* means 'to study', while *teach* means 'to instruct'.

like and **as** The use of the word *like* as a conjunction is good English, as you can see in the following examples: 'Anna is very *like* her mother', 'Bill plays the violin *like* a professional', 'This coin looks *like* silver to me'.

It is not good practice to use *like* as a preposition, such as in the sentence 'This room looks *like* it's been hit by a hurricane'. The correct phrase would read, 'This room looks *as if* it's been hit by a hurricane'.

ANNA IS VERY LIKE HER MOTHER

ENGLISH USAGE

livid and **angry** 'When I got to school yesterday, my teacher was *livid* because I was so late'. The word *livid* is often used to mean 'angry', but it originally meant 'of a greyish tinge or colour'.

mad This word means 'insane, or mentally deranged', but is often used to mean 'angry', particularly in the United States. The second use is an informal one, and is best avoided in written English.

majority This means 'the greater number'. It cannot be used to describe quantities or areas. It is therefore wrong to say: 'The *majority* of Europe was covered by snow'. Instead of *the majority*, you should say *most of*, or *the greater part*. However it is correct English to say: 'The *majority* of children are more healthy today' because children can be counted as separate things.

malapropism A *malapropism* is a word that sounds similar to another and is used wrongly in its place. It was named after Mrs Malaprop, a character in *The Rivals* by Sheridan. An example of a *malapropism* would be to use 'fertile' instead of 'futile' in the sentence: 'All our efforts are *fertile*'.

mantel and **mantle** The first word means 'the surround to a fireplace', while *mantle* means 'a loose wrap or cloak'.

masterful and **masterly** The first word means 'domineering', and the second means 'skilful'.

may and **might** The word *might* is the past tense of *may*. It expresses possibility in sentences like 'It *may* be fine tomorrow', 'You *might* have been hurt'. In both sentences, *may* could be exchanged for *might* and *might* for *may*, but the meanings of both sentences would be a little different. If I say '*Might* I take you out to dinner?', it sounds a little less certain than '*May* I take you out to dinner?', although both sentences are correct English.

maybe and **may be** The first word is an adverb and means 'perhaps or possibly', as in the sentence '*Maybe* I will be going to the theatre tonight'. *May be*, however, is two verbs, as in the sentence: 'My sister Clare *may be* coming to visit us tomorrow'.

media This word has come into use to describe methods of communication such as newspapers, television and radio and is, in fact, the plural of *medium*. It is therefore wrong to speak of *media* as if it were singular, as in: 'The *media* is responsible for much of the lack of discipline today'. The sentence should read 'The *media* are . . .'

mediocre This does not mean 'bad'. It means 'average or ordinary in quality; neither good nor bad'.

meter and **metre** The word *meter* is a device or machine for measuring something. A *metre* is a measurement of length. American custom uses the same spelling, *meter*, for both.

more and **most** It is wrong to say, for instance, 'Jack is the *most* intelligent of my two sons', because when comparing two things you should use the comparative *more*. You cannot have the *most* intelligent of two. However, you should use *most* when speaking of three or more, as in 'There are a lot of bookshops in London and *most* of them are in the West End'.

myself The word *myself* should not be used instead of 'I' or 'me'. The two following sentences are wrong: 'It was kind of you to ask my son and *myself* to your party', 'The members of the society and *myself* waited for a reply'. In the first sentence, *myself* should be replaced by *me*, and in the second, it should be replaced by *I*.

naught and **nought** The word *naught* means 'nothing', but the word *nought* refers to the zero symbol 0. The word *naughty* is taken from *naught*, and originally meant 'good for nothing'.

never means 'not ever' and it is wrong to use it if you are referring to only one occasion, as in 'I *never* met you on the train today'. This sentence should read: 'I did not meet you on the train today'. In the sentence, 'I have *never* been to the British Museum', the word *never* is used correctly.

No. or **no.** This is the standard abbreviation used in English and other European languages for the word *number*. In the United States, the symbol # is commonly used.

no one and **no-one** Either of these two forms can be used, but the two words should never be run together as *noone*.

not only . . . but also If you use the expression *not only* it must be balanced by *but also* later in the sentence. For example: 'Jane lost *not only* her scarf, *but also* her gloves', 'We would like *not only* to meet you, *but also* your friend'.

ENGLISH USAGE

noun A *noun* is the grammatical term for words which are the names of things, animals, ideas and qualities. There are four kinds of *nouns: proper nouns, abstract nouns, collective nouns* and *common nouns* (*see box for examples*).

A *proper noun* is a special name for a place, thing or person. All proper nouns take capital letters. The days of the week and months of the year are also *proper nouns*.

An *abstract noun* is something which cannot be actually touched, seen or physically felt.

Collective nouns are those which deal with collections of things or persons.

Common nouns include all the rest, a few examples being given here: *house, man, pencil, tree, plate, sky, wood, chalk, coffee, anvil.*

Nouns can sometimes be used as verbs. Here are some examples: 'Joe is going to *paper* his room', 'The engineer came to *service* our dishwasher', 'That is a nasty cut; let me *bandage* it'.

Nouns can also be used as adjectives, as in '*barber* shop', '*birthday* present', '*customer* service', '*soap*-dish'.

Nouns
proper nouns:
Australia
Memphis
New York
William Shakespeare
Shredded Wheat
The White House
Saturday
December

abstract nouns
kindness   truth
terror   pleasure
bravery   honesty
fear   fame
hope   happiness
love

collective nouns:
a swarm of bees
a herd of cattle
a gaggle of geese
a ship's crew
a fleet of ships
a company of actors
a school of dolphins
a football team
a band of robbers
a clump of trees
a pack of cards
a set of pencils
a litter of kittens
a cluster of trees
a troop of monkeys

occur and **take place** The word *occur* means 'to happen by chance', while *take place* is used when an event or occasion is prearranged. 'An accident *occurred* in the market square' illustrates the first, while 'The wedding will *take place* on Thursday' illustrates the use of the second phrase.

off of This expression is sometimes heard, as in 'I jumped *off of* the platform'. It is incorrect and the word *of* should be omitted.

official and **officious** *Official* means 'formal or authorized', while *officious* means 'interfering or meddlesome'.

ENGLISH USAGE

only It is important to place the word *only* correctly in a sentence, otherwise the meaning can be quite different. Here are some examples: 'Peter spoke *only* to Caroline' means that Peter spoke to Caroline and nobody else. '*Only* Peter spoke to Caroline' means that it was Peter and no-one else who spoke to Caroline. 'Peter *only* spoke to Caroline' means that Peter did nothing more than speak to Caroline.

-or and **-our** The ending *-our* is usual in such words as *honour, colour, labour, behaviour*. However, there are a number of exceptions. The following words are spelled *-or*: *error, horror, languor, liquor, pallor, squalor, stupor, terror, torpor, tremor*. In the United States, most *-our* ending words are spelled *-or*, but there are exceptions. The word *glamour* is spelled *-our* both in Britain and America.

oral and **aural** These two words are pronounced in almost exactly the same way, but they mean different things. *Oral* means 'spoken, verbal' or 'of the mouth', while *aural* means 'of the ear'. If you attend an *oral examination*, the questions and answers will be spoken out loud. An *aural test* will check your hearing.

outside of The word *outside* should not be followed by *of*. The word *of* should be omitted.

pail and **pale** The first word is a noun and means 'a bucket', and the second word is an adjective and means 'lacking brightness or colour'.

palate, **palette** and **pallet**. *Palate* means 'the roof of the mouth', a *palette* is 'an artist's board for mixing colours', and a *pallet* is 'a portable wooden platform' or 'an instrument used by potters'.

palindrome A *palindrome* is a word, phrase or number, which, if taken in reverse order, will read the same. Here are some palindromes: *Noon; nun; madam; mum; Bob; Madam, I'm Adam; Able was I ere I saw Elba; 1991.*

ENGLISH USAGE

participle *Participles* are parts of a verb, which are used, together with auxiliary verbs, to form tenses. A *participle* can also be used as an adjective. There are two kinds: *present participles* and *past participles*. Present participles end in *-ing*, as in *jumping, printing, turning, walking*. Past participles usually end in *-d* or *-ed*, as in *heard, jumped, printed, turned, walked*. Sometimes they end in *-n* or *-t*, as in *broken* and *burnt*.

You can use a *present participle* with the auxiliary verb 'to be', as in *I am jumping, he is printing, she was turning, they were walking*. You can use a *past participle* with the auxiliary verb 'to have', as in *I have jumped, he has printed, she has turned, they have walked*.

Participles can also be used as adjectives, as in 'the *burnt* paper', 'the *broken* cup', 'the *jumping* horse', 'the *printed* book', 'the *turning* wheel', 'the *walking* doll'.

passed and **past** *Passed* is a verb (the past tense of *pass*), and is used in such sentences as 'You have *passed* my house', 'Father has *passed* the age of sixty', 'Many years have now *passed*'. The word *past* can be a noun, an adjective or a preposition: 'History tells what happened in the *past*' [noun]; 'There has been very bad weather during the *past* week' [adjective]; 'The bus drove straight *past*' [preposition].

pedal and **peddle** A *pedal* is a lever operated by the foot, and *peddle* is a verb, and means 'to go from place to place selling things'.

peninsula and **peninsular**. The first word is a noun and means 'a piece of land almost surrounded by water'. The second word is an adjective and means 'of, or like, a peninsula'.

pidgin and **pigeon** The first word describes a kind of trading language used in the South Seas, and the second word describes a kind of bird.

perestroika This is a Russian word which has only recently come into the English language. It means 'reconstruction or reform'.

ENGLISH USAGE

plain and **plane** The first word, *plain*, means 'clear, distinct or straightforward', while *plane* can mean either 'a flat surface' or 'a kind of tree'. It is also used as an abbreviated version of 'aeroplane'.

plurals The *plural* in English (that is, when more than one person or thing is named) is usually formed by adding an *s* to the noun, as in: book, *books*; hand, *hands*; house, *houses*; tree, *trees*; way, *ways*. Words ending in *ch*, *s*, *sh*, *x*, and *z* add *es* for the *plural*, as in church, *churches*; loss, *losses*; bush, *bushes*; box, *boxes*; fizz, *fizzes*.

When a noun ends in *y* with a consonant before it, the *y* is changed to an *i*, as in baby, *babies*; lady, *ladies*; story, *stories*; company, *companies*; history, *histories*. If a vowel comes before the *y*, the *plural* usually remains as *s*, as in boy, *boys*; storey, *storeys*; tray, *trays*.

Most nouns ending with *f* or *fe* change the *f* or *fe* into *v* and add *es*, as in leaf, *leaves*; wolf, *wolves*; thief, *thieves*; wife, *wives*. There are exceptions; the following words keep the *f* and add an *s*: belief, *beliefs*; chief, *chiefs*; dwarf, *dwarfs*; reef, *reefs*; roof, *roofs*.

Common words ending in *o* take *es* as a *plural*, as in cargo, *cargoes*; potato, *potatoes*; hero, *heroes*; tomato, *tomatoes*; echo, *echoes*. There are many others, however, which simply add *s*: commando, *commandos*; dynamo, *dynamos*; piano, *pianos*; radio, *radios*.

There are some *irregular plurals*. Certain words, such as *deer, cod, sheep, salmon, aircraft, measles, scissors* remain the same, whether singular or *plural*. Some words form their *plural* by adding *en*, as in ox, *oxen*; child, *children*; man, *men*; woman, *women*. Yet other words become *plural* by changing the vowel or vowels in the middle of the word, as in foot, *feet*; tooth, *teeth*; goose, *geese*; mouse, *mice*.

possessive adjectives The *possessive* of an adjective shows who something or someone belongs to. It is formed by the use of the words *his, hers, its, my, our, their, your,* as used in such sentences as '*My* car has *its* difficulties', 'Where is *our* car?', 'I have met *your* friend', 'You must keep *your* temper'. The word *whose* is both a *possessive adjective* and a possessive pronoun, as in: 'The girl *whose* bicycle I borrowed is my friend' [possessive adjective]; and 'I borrowed a bicycle, but I didn't know *whose*' [possessive pronoun].

ENGLISH USAGE

possessive nouns The *possessive* form of a noun is usually shown by adding *'s* or *s'*. In the case of a single noun, add *'s*, as in *the boy's book, the girl's dress, Peter's house*. If the noun is singular, but ends in *s*, add *'s*, as in *the princess's tour, the rhinoceros's horn, the platypus's bill, St James's Square*.

Words ending in *x* or *z* are treated in the same way: *Max's restaurant, Liz's scarf*. If the noun is plural and ends in *s*, add an apostrophe only: *the teachers' room, the soldiers' uniforms*. If the noun is plural, but does not end in *s*, add *'s*, as in *the children's toys, the men's room, the women's club*. Words ending in *es* are treated as if they were plural nouns and only an apostrophe is added: *Moses' people*.

possessive pronouns The *possessive* of pronouns is formed by the use of the words: *hers, its, mine, ours, theirs, whose, yours,* as in 'That car is *theirs*', 'This pen is *mine*', 'Which dress is *hers*?'. An apostrophe is not used in these cases, so it is wrong to write: *her's, it's, our's, their's, who's, your's* [*it's* and *who's* mean *it is* and *who is*].

practicable and **practical** The first word means 'possible, feasible, able to be put into practice', and the second means 'workable, useful, adapted to actual conditions'.

pray and **prey** The word *pray* means 'to offer a prayer', and *prey* means 'an animal hunted for food'.

precede and **proceed** *Precede* means 'to go or come before', and *proceed* means 'to carry on, to progress'.

precedent and **president** The first word means 'an example or instance used in law', while the second means 'the head of a state, republic or company'.

prefix This is placed before a word to form a new word. The following are commonly used *prefixes*: *ex-* means 'out of' or 'former', as in *export*, or *ex-president*; *pre-* means 'before in time or position', as in *prehistoric*; *re-* means 'to return or do again' as in *return* or *rewind*; *un-* and *dis-* denote reversal of an action, as in *undress* and *disapprove*; *non-* denotes a negative, as in *non-member*. (See page 123.)

preposition A *preposition* is a word used with a noun (or the equivalent of a noun) to show the position or relation of the noun to other words (*see box for examples*). Sometimes, several words together can form a *preposition*, such as *with regard to; up to; in respect of; onto;*

THE RHINOCEROS'S HORN

ENGLISH USAGE

in accordance with. *Prepositions* link and introduce phrases, and show direction or relationship. 'Mr Brown realized that his wife was *out* of the house, and drove the car *into* town', 'I shall remain here *until* February'.

There is an old rule which says that a sentence should never end with a *preposition*. In fact, *prepositions* should go before the noun, but sometimes it is not possible to write a sentence without ending it with a *preposition*. Sir Winston Churchill made a joke of the rule by writing 'this is the sort of English *up with* which I will not put'.

Sentences ending with a *preposition* can be used when necessary but there are some which sound wrong. Here is one which ends with no fewer than three prepositions: 'What did you choose that book to be read *out of for*?'. If a sentence sounds wrong, it almost certainly *is* wrong.

principal and **principle** The word *principal* means 'chief, leading, main'

prepositions	
after	of
at	on
before	out
by	over
down	through
for	to
from	until
in	up
into	with

and the second word, *principle*, means 'a general truth, law or standard'.

prise and **prize** The first word is a verb and means 'to force open', while the second, as a noun, means 'a reward'. *Prize* can be a verb meaning 'to value greatly', and it can also be another spelling of the first word *prise*.

prone means 'lying face downward'.

pronoun A *pronoun* is a word used instead of, or to replace a noun. The following words are all *pronouns*: *I, me,*

ENGLISH USAGE

she, him, her, one, it, you, we, us, they, them. These are called *personal pronouns*. There are four other kinds: relative *pronouns – who, whose, whom, which, that*; possessive *pronouns – mine, yours, his, hers, its, ours, theirs*; interrogative *pronouns – what, who, which, whom, whose*; and demonstrative *pronouns – this, these, that, those, the other, others, such, the same.* (*See box.*)

---

pronouns

personal pronoun:
'Mr Smith owns a shop. *He* sells sweets.'

relative pronoun:
'Mr Smith is the owner of the shop *that* sells sweets.'

possessive pronoun:
'*His* sweet shop is very successful.'

interrogative pronoun:
'*Whose* shop is that and *what* does it sell?'

demonstrative pronoun:
'*This* shop belongs to Mr Smith.'

---

question mark [?] This is a mark of punctuation, and is used instead of a full stop at the end of direct 'question' sentences. *What is your name? How shall I get to your house? When will the next lesson be?* In dialogue, that is, when you are writing down someone's conversation, you should enclose the statement in quotation marks and include the *question mark* inside the quotation: '"*Would you like an ice-cream?*" asked Mary', '"*What time does the train leave?*" enquired Sam'. In these cases, the following word (*asked* and *enquired*) does not need a capital letter.

quiet and **quite** Although they are pronounced differently, these two words are sometimes confused. *Quiet* means 'calm and tranquil', and *quite* means 'completely and absolutely'.

quire and **choir** Both these words have a similar pronunciation, but are spelled differently. *Quire* is a measurement for a quantity of paper, and a *choir* is a group of singers.

quotation marks [' '] or [" "] These are used at the beginning and at the end of something that is quoted, such as conversation. *Quotation marks* are either single [' '] or double [" "] inverted commas. '"Don't be silly,' said Alice', '"What a lovely day!" exclaimed the March Hare'. The *quotation marks* are placed only at the beginning and end of the actual sentence or phrase quoted.

ENGLISH USAGE

SKULL SCULLING

raise and **raze** The first word is a verb meaning 'to move to a higher position', and the second word is also a verb, but means 'to demolish completely'.

rapt, **rapped** and **wrapped** *Rapt* is an adjective, and means 'totally absorbed or engrossed', *rapped* is a verb, the past tense of 'to rap', while *wrapped* is the past tense of the verb 'to wrap', and means 'to enfold or cover'.

recount and **re-count** The first word means 'to tell a story', and the second means 'to count again'.

redolent means 'odorous' or 'smelling of'.

reflexive pronouns The following are *reflexive pronouns: myself, yourself, himself, herself, oneself, itself, ourselves, yourselves, themselves.* They are used to refer to the subject of the clause or sentence in which they are found. Here are some examples: 'I ate the apples *myself*', 'he found *himself* back on the road', 'you can do that job *yourself*', 'we all enjoyed *ourselves*'.

reform and **re-form** The first word means 'to improve or correct', and the second word means 'to form anew'.

reign and **rein** To *reign* means 'to rule or exercise power', while a *rein* is 'one of a pair of straps used to control a horse'.

review and **revue** A *review* is a report or essay, but a *revue* is a theatrical performance.

rhyme and **rime** *Rhyme* means a word-ending which sounds like another, and *rime* means 'frost'. This last spelling was used once for both words.

said When you are writing dialogue, that is, words spoken by a character in a story, the style is usually like this: '"Please come in and sit down," *said* Mr Evans'. The word *said* can be used as many times as required but it can also be replaced by many other 'verbs of speaking', for example: *whispered, spluttered, smiled, grinned, shouted, called, asked, demanded, queried, replied, exclaimed, ordered, screamed, grumbled, complained, reminded.*

sceptic and **septic** The word *sceptic* means 'someone who distrusts or disbelieves people', while *septic* means 'infected by bacteria'. The first word is pronounced 'skeptic', which is the way the word is spelled in the United States.

scull and **skull** To *scull* means 'to row a boat', while *skull* means 'the bones of the head'.

ENGLISH USAGE

semi-colon [;] This is a punctuation mark. It is used when something stronger than a comma, but less strong than a full stop, is needed. Usually it is used to link two parts of a sentence which are not already linked by a conjunction, as in: 'The car wouldn't start; its battery was flat', 'The snow fell heavily; it covered roof-tops everywhere', 'The girl ran quickly; she wanted to escape'.

sew and **sow** The word *sew* means 'to use needle and thread', while *sow* means 'to scatter seed'.

simile *Similes* are figures of speech, in which one thing is compared with another, such as in *dead as a doornail; deaf as a post; mad as a hatter; red as a beetroot*. These are *similes*, but they are also clichés and best avoided. These are some more acceptable examples of *similes*: 'Her *cheek* was *like damask*; her *hair as* spun *gold*', 'As soon as Ben saw his angry father, he shot out of his *chair like a rocket*'.

stationary and **stationery** The first word means 'not moving, standing still', and the second word means 'writing materials'.

stile and **style** A *stile* is a set of steps over and through a fence, and *style* means 'form or appearance'.

storey and **story** The word *storey* means 'a floor or level of a building', and *story* means 'a tale or yarn'. The plural of *storey* is *storeys*; that of *story* is *stories*. In the United States, both words are usually spelled 'story'.

straight and **strait** The word *straight* means 'not curved or crooked', and the word *strait* means 'a narrow channel of the sea'.

suffix A *suffix* is placed at the end of a word to form a new one. Here are some *suffixes*: -able, -ible, -al, -ance, -dom, -ful, -ish, -less, -ment, -ness. The following are some examples of words using the *suffixes* mentioned: *liable, sensible, usual, kingdom, thoughtful, boyish, fearless, payment, silliness*. There is a large number of *suffixes*, each one of which has a special purpose to change the meaning of a noun (*see page 126*).

swam and **swum** The word *swam* is the past tense of the verb to *swim*, and is used as in the sentence: 'Dick *swam* across the river'. The word *swum* should not be used in such a way, since it is a *past participle* and needs the auxiliary verb 'to have'. Here is an example of its use: 'Several people *had swum* across the lake'.

synonyms	
abbreviate	shorten
abundant	plentiful
apparition	ghost
attire	dress
begin	commence
bravery	courage
brief	short
choice	option
conclusion	ending
courteous	polite
difficult	hard
enemy	foe
hatred	loathing
huge	enormous
inside	interior
rarely	seldom
sly	cunning
suspend	hang
thankful	grateful
unite	join

synonym A *synonym* is a word which has a similar, or closely related meaning to another word (*see box*). English words do not have exact *synonyms*, although some are very close in meaning to others. The word *fast*, for instance, means almost the same as *quick* but the two words cannot always be interchanged. You would speak of a '*fast* car', but not of a '*quick* car'.

tautology means unnecessary repetition of an idea. Here are some examples: 'Sally has drawn a *four-sided square* on her paper'. All squares are four-sided, so the words 'four-sided' should be omitted. 'Everyone knows that Columbus discovered America. It's *past history!*' History is in the past anyway, so the word 'past' is not needed. 'A *free gift* with every new bike!' A gift is something given free of charge therefore you do not need the word 'free'. Here are a few expressions commonly used, but which are *tautological:* added bonus; all alone; check up; close down; divide up; end result; finish up; later on; over again; refer back; settle up; true facts; unite together.

their, **there** and **they're** The first word means 'belonging to them', and the second means 'in that place', while the third is a contraction of the two words *they are*.

times and dates It is very important, when writing down a *time* or a *date*, that the reader should be in no doubt as to its meaning. *Times* should be clear: *9 a.m.* (not *9.00 a.m.*), *10.30 p.m., half-past six, five o'clock*. If the 24-hour clock is used, then *times* should be shown as: *9.00 hrs., 11.30 hrs., 18.20 hrs., 23.10 hrs. Dates* should be clear, too. The simplest method is *date, month, year*, as in *14 October 1978*. It is best to avoid writing *dates* in the form *12/10/89* or *12.10.89*. In Great Britain, this would be read as: *12 October, 1989*, but in the United States it would be read as: *December 10, 1989*.

tire and **tyre** The word *tire* means 'to become fatigued or weary', and *tyre* means 'the rim of a wheel'. In the United States the first spelling is used for both words.

troop and **troupe** The word *troop* is used to describe a unit in an army, while *troupe* is applied to a group of actors or performers.

unique means 'the only one of its kind, without equal or like', so you cannot say *almost unique, fairly unique* or *quite unique*.

unwanted and **unwonted** The first word means 'not wanted', and the second means 'unusual or out of the ordinary'.

verb A *verb* is a part of speech which asks a question, expresses a command, and tells what someone or something does or is. *Verbs* can tell you about the past, in the past tense, the present, in

ENGLISH USAGE

the present tense, and the future, in the future tense. Here is a *verb*, showing the parts of speech and the three tenses:

Present	Past	Future
I jump	I jumped	I will jump
You jump	You jumped	You will jump
He jumps	He jumped	He will jump
She jumps	She jumped	She will jump
We jump	We jumped	We will jump
They jump	They jumped	They will jump

Verbs are divided into transitive and intransitive *verbs*. A transitive *verb* always needs an object; it does something *to* something. For example the *verb* 'to hit' is a transitive *verb*; you must hit something, 'I *hit* the floor'. Intransitive *verbs* do not require an object. The *verb* 'to sleep' is intransitive, since you cannot *sleep* anything; you just sleep.

Auxiliary *verbs* are 'helping' *verbs*; they are used with other *verbs*. The usual auxiliary *verbs* are *to be*, *to have* and *to do*. Here are some examples of auxiliary *verbs*: '*I am* walking to Oxford in aid of Oxfam', 'Those boxes *are* not wanted on the voyage', 'She *has* asked me to call round this evening', 'I *do* not wish to be disturbed'.

waive and **wave** *Waive* means 'to set aside, or to give up something', and *wave* means 'to flutter, or signal with something'.

wander and **wonder** The word *wander* means 'to move about in an irregular way', while *wonder* means 'something strange or exciting', but it is also a verb which means 'to ponder or think about'.

yoke and **yolk** The word *yoke* means 'a wooden neck-piece for oxen', and *yolk* means 'the yellow part of an egg'.